IN SEARCH OF THE

GOLDEN NUGGETS

THE KEYS TO WORK, WISDOM AND WEALTH

By
Enid Vien

A DYNAMISM PUBLICATION

Enid Vien

In Search of the Golden Nuggets
Copyright © 2000 by Enid Vien

Inquiries should be addressed to:

Dynamism Publications
PO BOX 242,
La Mesa, CA. 91944-0242

ISBN # 0-9648330-6-9

First Edition 2000
First Printing 2000

Printed in the United States of America
By Morgan Printing, Austin, Texas.

COVER ART by Stephen Bright.

IN SEARCH OF THE GOLDEN NUGGETS

PREAMBLE

When embarking on a book such as this one, it becomes necessary to examine one's qualifications to expound on the subject. Why should you, or any one else for that matter, listen to me?

Actually, you shouldn't. You can study and consider what I say, but I think it is better that you listen to yourself while reading it. If my work strikes a chord with you, then I will have done my job well.

Since early childhood I have been fascinated by humanity and the human condition; by what makes us tick. When other kids were still playing with dolls, I was reading my way through the shelves of the local library, passionately inhaling everything I could find on philosophy, religion, psychology and every other related subject I could find. I was looking for the answers to why it was that the grown ups felt it necessary to drop bombs on each other, why people found it necessary to attack and hate. (Growing up, as I did, in war torn London, had made these questions intensely important to me.)

I have dedicated my life and spent thousands of hours studying people, since the point when I decided the books did not contain the knowledge I was seeking. Thirty some years ago I became a Clearing Practitioner, minister and coach. This offered me a way to help people free up their life energy in order for them to stay at peak performance.

During these thirty years I have worked with, and had the opportunity to study, people from all backgrounds. I have trained other practitioners and guided thousands of individuals to greater success in fields as varied as homemaker to tycoon.

I have spent the past ten years developing Dynamism's special clearing procedures, and have written several books on the theories behind clearing.

In short, people are my passion, my inspiration and my field of expertise. The same principles, that I have used for so many years to improve life in general, can be applied equally well to business and success. This became very clear when people began calling me the millionaire maker. At first I found this odd because my ideas were all along the lines of becoming more spiritual and less materialistic. Then I took another look and I saw that one could apply many of the principles I teach to a wide spectrum of activities, including business.

In 1967, when I first came to the USA, the average family could still get by on one income. The American Dream was attainable for a family that worked hard and spent wisely. There was a surplus of goods and money flowed quite freely. Gasoline was cheap and the economy was healthy. The atmosphere was one of prosperity and optimism. Today, in 2000, the financial climate has distinctly changed. Most families have to have two incomes just to stay even with the expenses.

Getting ahead takes far more ability to achieve. Simply working hard is no longer adequate to ensure financial stability, let alone success. It has become necessary to understand certain principles of management, marketing and marketplaces just to compete in the competitive clamor that exists in the business world today.

This is still the land of opportunity, but now you must create it and not wait around for it to find you.

Happy Hunting,

Enid Vien

Acknowledgments

First I must mention Dr. Bruce Crawford who *demanded* that I write this book. Secondly, I am indebted to Robert and Kim Kiyosaki, Diane Kennedy and Dr. Van Tharp whose inspiring ideas helped keep me writing it. I must not forget to mention Homer Wilson Smith for his insightful ideas on competition, along with Ken and Angela Payne for their tremendous support. There's a wealth of others, you know who you are.

For the proofreaders, the cover art, the editing and all the usual nuts and bolts that go into the production of a book, thanks go to Suzanne Camper, James Hollingsworth and all the usual helpers at Morgan Printing.

All such lengthy tasks take their toll on one's personal life and I must thank my husband, David Womack, for answering phones, keeping the doors open and fending off distractions. This is a thankless task usually, because I only notice those distractions that fall through the cracks and interrupt me.

Enid Vien

FOREWORD

I love the title of this book.

From ancient days, man has gone off in far-ranging quests. He has faced physical, emotional and mental challenges to the point of death. He braves all this in search of the elusive golden nugget.

Yet, the journey for these prized golden nuggets doesn't really force us to travel an exotic land fraught with danger, author Enid Vien assures us. Instead the journey is one within ourselves.

As we gain the skills and insights to harness the energy and vitality each one of us has – the "Dynamis" – our lives will never be the same. *In Search of the Golden Nuggets* is a practical guide for releasing that energy and gaining the confidence to face life again with hope and a sense of future.

From a practical viewpoint, both as a practicing Certified Public Accountant in the U.S., and as a client of Enid Vien, I know personally what gaining that joy can mean. I have seen other clients free themselves, with Enid's help and guidance, to accomplish what they hardly dared hope before. One client increased his business ten fold in one year. Another client tells of merely "thinking" about a goal and somehow it is achieved with little or no effort.

Logically, it makes sense that would be so. If you can increase your focus, gain confidence, increase available energy and free yourself from unwanted patterns, how could you not be more successful in everything you want to achieve? And, once your current goals are achieved and needs met, what more can you do with your life?

That is what it means to find golden nuggets. Those golden nuggets are within each of us and available. This book will be a stepping-stone on the way to achieving all you want. Have a wonderful journey!

Diane Kennedy, CPA
Phoenix, Arizona
May 2000

Recommended Reading

Philosophy of Finances:

"Rich Dad, Poor Dad"
By Robert Kiyosaki and Sharon Lechter CPA

"The Cash Flow Quadrant"
By Robert Kiyosaki and Sharon Lechter CPA

Trading:

"Trade Your Way to Financial Freedom"
By Dr. Van Tharp

Corporate Information and Tax Strategies:

"Inc. & Grow Rich"
By Diane Kennedy CPA

"Rich in America – How to Use Your Business to Pay Less Taxes"
By Diane Kennedy CPA

TABLE OF CONTENTS

AUTHOR'S NOTE

This book is designed so it can also be used as a workbook. There are exercises after each chapter. If you chose to do them please feel free to send us your comments and hopefully tell us of your wins and gains. Our website has e-mail addresses and our PO Box is: Dynamism Publications, PO Box 242, La Mesa, CA. 91941

Chapter One
GOLDEN NUGGETS

Sometimes it seems I have spent my entire life in search of the Golden Nuggets. I have been fascinated with the idea that when you find your own Golden Nuggets you open the door to your dreams.

Life in London when I was a young girl seemed to me to lack sparkle. There were so many people living in one area yet most of them never really touching each other in any meaningful way, scads of people. You could look at the faces and see their quiet and bitter suffering, their terrible emptiness. I did not want to spend my life that way. There had to be more to life than bare survival, more than 30 years with the company and a shiny gold watch, more than a couple of kids and a big mortgage, more than war and endurance. When I visited my Yorkshire relatives the nearest town was a mining community with a gray pall of coal dust everywhere. The people were gray, the sky was gray, and the mood was gray. These miners and their families lived under the sword of Damocles every day of their dreary existence. There were many cripples in the town; injured in mine cave-ins. My Aunt told me that black lung was a scourge too.

There had to be an upside. This could not be all there was to life.

On the other hand there were people I had read about who seemed to shine. Men like Picasso and Gaugin, following their brilliant stars, particularly appealed to me, but there were others like Norma Shearer, Isadora Duncan, (both dancers) there was Dickens and Kipling, there was Albert Schweitzer and Albert Einstein. These people felt inspirational to me. They were unusual in their talents, unusual in their zest for their chosen subjects, larger than life, magical in their intensity. I began to think of this as having found their Golden Nuggets. The concept was that of the perfectly beautiful and shiny item that was SO valuable that it spurred one into action in order to gain or achieve it.

Somewhere along the way I realized that the key to my own Golden Nuggets involved helping others to find their Nuggets. Also somewhere along the line it became clear that one can have many Golden Nuggets not just one. Back then I was thinking of them as external to self, now I know that they are within one's heart and spirit all along. Searching externally for one's inspiration is one thing, creating what the external object inspired is quite another.

This book is an attempt to bring together a lot of the wisdom I have collected through the years and share it with you.

We all have our dreams of success, of wealth and position. Some of us go through life chasing our dreams, looking for that pot of gold under the rainbow, panning streams for those Golden Nuggets. Some of us settle for half a loaf. Many of us spend our time bemoaning our fate.

Some lucky individuals have the Midas Touch, everything they do turns to gold, while others cannot hang on to a dime. What IS this phenomenon? Why do some people have the lucky touch, when others always seem to lose their wallets?

Nobody wants to be a loser, moaning and groaning about their latest hard luck story, however even those who chug along being marginally successful often wonder: What is the secret to success that the movers and shakers of this world have discovered? Actually, I do not believe that there is ONE secret to success. Success comes from hard work that is intelligently applied to produce desirable or useful products that can be sold at a profit. Wealth comes from applying the fruits of success to investments that generate income.

When we are children we are usually taught certain values, one of which is that: "Hard Work brings its own reward." Later we come to realize that we have only been taught part of the puzzle. We work hard and we expect our just reward, but it is not always forthcoming. After we have accumulated enough disappointments, often we abandon our high goals and settle down to a life of monotonous compromise. This weakens us and frequently our unfulfilling existence becomes increasingly burdensome. The sparkle leaves our eyes and we wait, just getting by from week to week, year to year, hanging on for our retirement where (we hope) we can finally get to do some of the things we *really* want to do: travel, putter in the garden, catch up on our reading, or watch TV all day. Thus the childhood dreams evaporate into one more life of dreary mediocrity.

Not a very attractive picture!

Some of us keep striving for success, prospecting for those golden nuggets, but more of us by far, live lives of quiet desperation. Desperate because, in our heart of hearts we know we are failing to reach our full potential. Locked into our selected compromise, doing the things we think are necessary to survive, we take no risks that are not carefully weighed and measured. Some others, while appearing to be doing well, still have not yet found their fulfillment. A few, very few, are out their actively finding new markets to conquer, new horizons to explore, new dragons to slay.

Clearly there is a difference in the thought processes of those who fail, those who struggle along, those who just get by, those who manage well, and those who turn lead into gold. It certainly looks like magic! These are the alchemists of the marketplace, the sorcerers to whom we long to apprentice ourselves.

There really is a special magic to it. It is the magic that comes from within the individual. Unlocking YOUR intrinsic magic, learning to live at peak performance and developing the Midas touch is not only possible, it is essential if one wants to live a fulfilling life.

Like all worthwhile things, there is a price to be paid. The price is:

1. Commitment.
2. Consistency.
3. Persistence.
4. Willingness to change
5. Ruthless self-examination.

To change any existing condition, it is first necessary to change your attitude towards it.

To change your attitude, it is first necessary to change the patterns of your thinking. This can be very difficult depending on how attached you are to your comfortable mental ruts. Some people believe that changing one's ideas requires admitting they were wrong; this idea is a trap. Change in the face of rapidly changing markets, when well thought out, is not only lucrative, it is also a sign that someone is in tune with those changes and can predict the needs and desires of their customers. If your ideas and habits were in fact wrong for the changing times then surely it is better to be right NOW.

Each of us has, at some point in the past, committed ourselves to the mindset that we are currently using to run our lives, our businesses and our organizations. If our lives, businesses and organizations are not being wildly successful despite hard work or heroic efforts, then we must admit that there has to be something that could stand re-examination and some changes. It can be very difficult to evaluate the basis for one's decisions and actions, for it is the rock on which we have taken our stand. Doing so requires a considerable amount of courage and fortitude. It is a peculiarity of the very successful people whom I have known, they all display willingness and a capacity to keep constantly looking at those things that do or do not work at any given time. This makes it possible for them to cast out the unworkable and strengthen the workable. Doing this takes a definite decision to free one's mind of old ideas, and to simply study the current situation, with a willingness to continually re-examine one's findings as time flows along.

Any successful business and product began as an idea, a thought; it was somebody's brainchild. A thought is, of course, intangible. The intangible idea becomes a solid reality through planning and hard work. These are some of the remaining pieces of our previously mentioned puzzle. Any successful venture starts off as an intangible idea that then goes through various stages to finally emerge as a product. Once one has the product, one then has to consider marketing it, but I am getting ahead of my scheduled topic here.

We can only create those things we believe we can create. Otherwise we would never bother to get the project off the ground. We have to have the initial idea plus the idea that it is feasible and realistic to do it. So, everything that actually comes into existence is really only able to be created because somebody thought he could do it in the first place. When this sense of certainty is combined with the intelligence to designate the correct marketplace and the ability to communicate the value of the product to that marketplace in an adequate fashion, you have a potentially successful concept.

Ideas seem as though they have power, in reality they can do not hing of their own volition. An idea has no power of its own. Someone, a real live person, has to commit to the idea and bring it alive; bring it into existence in the world. Like a parked car, ideas sit and gather dust until a live person turns the ignition key. It takes someone in the driver's seat to get something rolling. The individual puts his life energy, his power, into the idea and gives it life.

How much life and longevity an idea has will depend on a number of factors:

It must be timely.

It must strike a chord of need or desire.

It must be advertised or in some way communicated to the correct segment of society (The one that needs and wants it.)

It must be correctly priced to make a profit and yet still sell.

The old jokes about selling ice to Eskimos or coals to Newcastle are very illustrative of the third factor. In today's noisily competitive society, a brilliant idea with an excellent product can still fail because the marketer targeted the wrong segment of society or released it into the market at the wrong time or in the wrong season.

Let us assume you have a good basic idea or ideas. You have a good product or service, fairly priced. What then is the difference between the person who rises to the occasion and becomes wildly successful and the one who does not? Further, why do some people experience tremendous peaks and valleys? Why do some people work themselves half to death, spinning their wheels and getting nowhere?

Kismet, "Lady Luck" or the capricious God of Chance are false answers. They take us down the Primrose Path to nowhere and hopelessness. Those who succeed drive their vehicle towards success rather than sit around hoping for a perfect wave or a lucky windfall. Not to say that windfalls are undesirable, it is just that the nature of windfalls is unpredictable.

An acquaintance of mine is always wailing that if it were not for bad luck he'd have no luck at all. Having studied his actions for quite some time, it is more than obvious to me that he is actively creating his "Bad Luck." He, with unerring and astonishing accuracy, manages to do all the wrong things, with the wrong people, at the wrong time. He *believes* life deals him rotten hands. This belief prevents him from any form of self-examination. It also places him at the effect of any chance wind that blows, for he is saying that he has no responsibility for the things that happen to him. He gets my vote for "Most unlikely to succeed." He has set the stage and written the script for failure, and left in it no spaces where personal success could exist.

All of us have life energy, it is how we use it, how much of it is available for our use, where and when we apply it, and perhaps the most important of all, how much we desire to use it – demanding success of ourselves, that defines the story. It determines the script that we write for our lives.

The Golden Nuggets are the little surprises, the magical moments of new awareness which, while they are intangible, they also open the door-

Enid Vien

way to success. They are found in the oddest places at times, and can easily be overlooked. How many times have you said, "I should have listened to myself?" Golden Nuggets are the keys to work, wisdom and wealth. In the final sense, we are our own Golden Nuggets, not the toys and trappings that come from success.

We all have our Golden Nuggets, they are like little keys that bring us to the "Aha's," those marvelous moments of clarity when we see our way clearly through the fog, and which get us back on the right road when we have lost our way.

6

Exercises for Chapter One

1. Give several examples of Golden Nuggets:

_____
_____
_____
_____
_____
_____
_____
_____
_____
_____
_____
_____

2. Write 3 examples you have seen where ventures failed for lack of consistency:

_____
_____
_____
_____
_____
_____
_____
_____
_____
_____
_____

3. Write 3 examples you have seen where business ventures failed due to lack of commitment:

_____
_____
_____
_____
_____
_____
_____
_____
_____

_____
_____

4. Write several examples of products that were successful because they were well marketed:

_____
_____
_____
_____
_____
_____
_____
_____
_____

5. What is the correct target for marketing a product?

_____
_____
_____
_____
_____
_____
_____
_____
_____
_____
_____

6. Give three examples of areas of your life that you would like to change:

_____
_____
_____
_____
_____
_____
_____
_____

7. Take each of these ideas and examine any ideas that you have that would need to change first:

Chapter Two
LIFE ENERGY

How often have you heard the complaint "I just can't find enough energy?" It seems to be a common occurrence. Physical fatigue and mental burnout form a pair, they go hand in hand. There is even a new illness that the Doctors call "chronic fatigue syndrome." Because they had no explanation for it, they simply gave it a nice important-sounding fancy name. Nevertheless many people suffer from exhaustion, they go to bed tired, and get up equally tired. It is difficult to get out of bed. No amount of vitamins, minerals or tonics, seem to help for very long. Life itself has become tiring and tiresome.

There is physical energy and non-physical life energy. The non-physical seems to be senior, in as much as we always seem to be able to find the energy for the things we really *want* to do.

Every living person has an energy that is uniquely their own. I call this energy Dynamis. It derives from the same Greek word that gives us dynamo and dynamic. Originally, it was believed by the Greeks that each God emanated a specific energy and the objects dedicated to that God were stamped or imprinted with that power. So, wine had the Dynamis of the God of Revelry and arrows that of the God of War, or the Goddess of the Hunt.

I chose to use the word Dynamis because we all have our own special energy and we leave our personal mark on the things we create or touch.

When you encounter a very creative and successful person you can sense their energy flowing from them in a focused stream of attention. They strike you as vigorous and powerful, and they would tend to draw you along in their enthusiastic approach to whatever task is at hand. Such individuals exude confidence and this confidence inspires others, lifting them up and adding to whatever power they already have.

Less successful individuals emanate a Dynamis that is not as clear; it is less focused and less powerful. Their brilliance is somewhat dulled and their energy does not catch you up and carry you along with them.

Some people seem born to be drones, chugging along, producing good work that keeps body and soul together, but never able to make much above the essentials.

There are even people whose energy is actively destructive, negating any positive results that those around them may be creating.

This is actually a descending scale of productive energy. We are all somewhere on this scale, with our Dynamis flowing freely or blocked to some degree. Success requires our energy flow to be strong and productive. Dynamism is the study of life energy and the development of methods to help you remove the barriers that impede your natural ability to flow strongly.

Each of us has a natural supply of life energy that diminishes as it becomes dammed up by adversity and painful experiences. These experiences imprint their effect on the individual who changes his attitude to life based on their impact. He carries forward the new conclusions, decisions and resolutions he made at that time in the hopes of avoiding future pain. Each such event is a turning point that lessens his flow of life energy from that time forward. They leave a bad taste in his mouth, a lingering sense that life may not be his oyster after all.

This applies to all areas of life, not just business. Losses, betrayals, wounds, setbacks; all leave scars on the soul. The person's spirit is wounded, sometimes even broken, by the time he is middle aged.

Knowing that he cannot dwell on it, the individual licks his wounds a bit, then stuffs the painful memory away in the special mausoleum in his mind erected for just this purpose, picks himself up and carries on with life. The strong feelings in the incident are really too much for him and thinking about it is too distressing and debilitating to contemplate. So, slamming the door firmly on the episode, he makes policies for himself hoping to prevent such things from ever happening to him again. His attitude has now changed. He has gone from eager to somewhat wary, from a free flow to a guarded one. In the future he will act more conservatively and with less spontaneity. He has substantially increased his chances of failure.

Even though the memory is buried, its effects remain. Along with his natural free energy he is now flowing some caution and distrust into the world around him. This affects everything he touches with its subtle influence. Other people sense the distrust and react to it. When, in the course of living, a person accumulates enough wounds to drastically alter his natural optimism and he becomes sour and embittered, those around him can become poisoned with the taint of his emanations. Misery is contagious. Fortunately for us, so is happiness.

Most of us have some sensitivity to the "vibes" of the people with whom we come in contact. They feel good or unpleasant or deceptive and we say we have a "gut" reaction to them. We are, in fact, sensing their Dynamis emanations.

Because our personal Dynamis does leave traces on the things we produce or are involved in, it actually has a major impact on our success or failure and so does the energy of those with whom we associate and work. A miserable sourpuss will drip his gloom and doom on all those he contacts. A cheerful soul will donate their cheerfulness to the world. A Pretender will give you a false sense of security. This tells us that choosing our companions in business has a great impact on our working environment. Although attitudes do change somewhat from day to day, due to the current events in our lives, like an unexpected bonus, or a death in the family, everyone has a "home base," a place on the Scale of Productive Energy [1] to which they return. This basic attitude is the one that seems to be the rock on which they stand. Observing someone for a while will usually help you to spot him or her correctly on this scale.

This gives you a fighting chance of choosing the right partner in an enterprise, or of selecting the clients with whom you wish to work, of deciding the best person to hire or fire, and can make your daily routine far more productive.

Looking through your client base usually discloses that there is a small section of clients on the list that account for a surprisingly high amount of trouble and which eats up a large block of your valuable time, while producing very little actual business. These clients will be found to correspond with the lower levels of the scale.

Simply choosing your teammates or employees wisely enormously increases your chances of success. Productivity increases, and the general atmosphere takes on a new, more optimistic flavor.

---

[1] See Scale of Productive Energy at the end of this Chapter.

If you take the idea that you can almost always find the energy for the things you really want to do as true, then it would logically follow that chronic exhaustion must have something to do with NOT doing the things you really want to do.

Not doing the things you really want can be because you have not sorted out exactly what you *do* want to do, or it can be from having too much opposition and distraction from those around you. When the latter is the case you may very well find yourself muttering or even yelling: "I am sick and tired of this." If the condition goes on too long, you may very well really get both sick and tired. This is especially true when you think your employees and teammates are helping, when in fact among them is a source of hidden trouble, a person who is instinctively or even deliberately making things go wrong. It is difficult to look at this for nobody wants to believe anyone could be destructive. Yet playing the ostrich[2] is almost as destructive, for it sours our dreams and breaks our backs under the burden of frustration that such people inspire. So, if you find yourself overloaded, irritable and are tired of dealing with mysterious yet continuous problems, this chart is well worth a lot of diligent study. In order to use it well you will find it necessary to inspect and classify lots of people until spotting where they fall on the chart becomes part of your thinking.

---

[2] Playing the ostrich: sticking one's head in the sand and refusing to look.

SCALE OF PRODUCTIVE ENERGY

ATTITUDE	POWER	PRODUCTIVITY
Enthusiasm "Let's GO!"	Strong Outward Flow	Excellent -- Go Getter
Cheerful "Let's get the Show on the Road."	Fairly strong Outflow	Willing to get on with it
Interested "I think we can do this."	Fairly Strong Outflow	Can learn and act.
Careful "Let us do some more research."	Cautious Outflow	Won't rock the boat.
Disinterested "You want me to do what?"	Little Flow	Capable but no dynamo
Aggressive "If it won't work, kick it."	Stops Other's Flows	Good when alone
Hostile "If you say so."	Begrudging Slow Flow	Produces only under duress
Pained "On top of everything else.."	Strong Flow Compulsive.	Works as if Driven. Makes Errors.
Rage "If it doesn't obey...Shoot it!"	Forceful Outflow	Breaks Equipment Uses lots of effort to produce little
Hateful "I hate this job."	Strong Destructive Out-flow.	As little as possible.
Hidden Rage "Everything is fine. Have a nice day."	Secret Destructive Flows.	Says it is done when it is not. Hides or destroys vital papers.
Pretender "I am the reason this place doesn't go broke."	Circular Flows that go no-where.	Looks very busy and successful. Produces lots of useless stuff. Wastes time and money.
Anxious / Fearful "I don't know if we can do it."	Scattered Flows.	Paper shuffler. Poor concentration. Gives boss little presents.
Bitterness "Nothing I do turns out right."	Stuck Flows.	Always has mysterious delays or problems.
Regret/Sorrow "I wish I was as good as I used to be."	Introverted -- self-absorbed flows.	Poor concentration. Apologizes a great deal.
Depressed "It's impossible."	Very introverted self ab-sorbed Flows.	Cannot concentrate on anything positive. Fixates on disaster.
Oppressed. "They are setting me up."	Cannot stop other's Flows.	Robotic. Produces only when given very specific orders.

Exercises for Chapter Two

1. Give three examples of things you do that you dislike doing:

   _____
   _____
   _____
   _____
   _____
   _____
   _____
   _____
   _____
   _____
   _____

2. Note how you feel when you make yourself do them:

   _____
   _____
   _____
   _____
   _____
   _____
   _____

3. Give three examples of things you love to do:

   _____
   _____
   _____
   _____
   _____
   _____
   _____
   _____

4. Note how you feel when you do them:

   _____
   _____
   _____
   _____

_____

_____

5. Look over the chart of Productive Energy and place the
    people you know in the correct categories. Make notes:

_____

_____

_____

_____

_____

_____

_____

_____

_____

_____

_____

_____

_____

_____

_____

_____

_____

_____

_____

_____

_____

_____

_____

_____

6. Re-examine your placing and make any needed adjust-
    ments:

_____

_____

_____

_____

_____

_____

_____

_____

_____

Chapter Three
COMMITMENT

Often we are told that we must "commit" to a project or business in order for it to succeed, yet it is not always wise or even possible to do so. Committing too strongly to a cause in which one has no real belief or interest can be tremendously soul destroying. To commit too strongly to a business path that is no longer appropriate to the changing market place can be disastrous. Commitment can all too easily become stubbornness.

Each person has their own unique set of desires and values. A goal that is of great importance to one person may seem dull and uninteresting to another. When a person is working towards a goal that is a true goal for him, the work seems effortless, easy and interesting. Obstacles are seen more as challenges than problems. Your true goals are some of your Golden Nuggets; they unlock the gate to personal productivity and pleasure.

True goals are those that flow out from the individual so naturally that he hardly has to think about them. It is goals such as these that are vital to success. They come from the basic purpose of the individual. Having a true goal makes it easy to commit. Simply stated, you *want* to do it. When you have been swerved away from your true purpose and your natural affinities by the influences of others, you are always fighting an uphill battle, trying to fit into shoes of the wrong size.

Joe wanted to be a fine artist but he allowed his mother to persuade him that dentistry was more sensible. She argued for security, for a recession-proof profession, and he fell for the concept because he was uncertain whether he could survive as an artist. He hates dentistry but is locked into it by debts and bills. In dentistry, he feels like a fish in a tree. He wistfully speaks of going to art school when he retires. This is an example of a person who is off-purpose. By off-purpose I mean following a goal that is not in alignment with his true purpose. He went for dentistry because it made sense and he has done fairly well at it, but it will never be his golden nugget. It will never take him to the dizzy heights of creativity to which he once aspired. Essentially he betrayed himself because of his doubts, he did not believe in his talent strongly enough to take the risk.

A person that selects a profession that does not thrill him, ring his bell and get his creative juices flowing will never get much pleasure from his work. Working just for security is drudgery at best.

Great success comes from going in the direction of those things that really appeal to you. This means you have to take a look at them and acknowledge the attraction. What is the major goal that is to your mind the most worthwhile thing you could possibly accomplish? Once you have sorted this out then all lesser goals can be examined and judged by how well they align to the main one. If you have swerved too far off your own purpose, finding it again can require considerable thought. It is worth doing because it gives you a rudder with which to steer your boat through life.

There are many laudable goals that are seductively worthwhile, but if they are not truly your goals, they will not do the trick. We all get good at those things we enjoy doing, no one has to force a brilliant pianist to practice, just try to stop him. He has his golden nugget. You want to find your golden nugget, the one that utilizes your natural talents and desires. It feels right and you just naturally gravitate towards it.

Most of us *think* too much and *do* too little. The habit of second-guessing ourselves can be utterly paralyzing. All those past failures and the insidious beliefs we formed at those times regarding our personal short-comings lead us into this pattern of introversion. The baggage from the past is affecting our attitude to the present. It is also a symptom of being off-purpose.

Some of us think too little and do too much, throwing money and energy down sinkhole projects that have not been well planned and which are usually also off-purpose. As though a project can be made to succeed, just by pouring effort into it.

When people are off-purpose it is hard for them to focus. They have to concentrate in order to direct their attention to their work because it is not where their attention would naturally go. This gives them a problem. It sets up an internal struggle that ties up a tremendous amount of their life energy. Due to this inner conflict, they will tend to collect little failures, things that would not have happened had they been able to pay full attention to their project at hand. These minor failures add up over time, and can be quite crippling to the will as well as very hard on the self-esteem.

Careful examination of the things that influenced you in making the major decisions that took you away from your major purpose in life will bring to light the individuals who had an impact on your thinking. Placing these individuals on the Scale of Productivity will enable you to see what type of influence each of them had. It is a very good idea to notice to WHOM one is listening, and to decide which influences, and who's, one wishes to have. A person who casts further doubt by strengthening your own reservations, for example, can really color your perception. Someone who *always* agrees with your more hair-brained schemes is also likely to have a poor sort of influence. Too much agreement *or* disagreement can have an unbalancing effect on your judgment.

The human race contains an extraordinarily high number of self-appointed critics who love giving advice on every subject imaginable, while never personally taking the leap of faith that it takes to really DO something. They seem to prefer offering advice on topics that they have not personally applied or studied. At the opposite end of the spectrum is the chronic admirer who considers you can do no wrong. Between these two poles is every conceivable variation of persons, all of whom have opinions.

If you want to be successful, by all means listen, but make your own decisions while taking all data and opinion into account. The one thing that is usually not factored into the "opinion equation," is the production level of the individual speaking. If this person is a "Don't rock the boat" type, expect conservative, cautious advice. If it is a Pretender, expect flowery gushes of praise. Using this Scale, one can predict the type of opinion and advice the individual will trot out for your inspection. People love to have their opinions considered and consulted, it is often a good way to keep your staff happy, but this does not mean you are obliged to follow their directives.

Anyone in a leadership position eventually realizes that he is the place where the buck stops. Some people find this uncomfortable and so delegate as many decisions as they can to others. If you have this tendency then it will be a tremendous aid for you to carefully spot the location on the Scale of Productivity for each person you put in positions of responsibility. Ultimately, the responsibility for decisions falls on the leader, so even when you are not making the individual daily decisions, you chose the people who do, which brings it home to you once again.

So much of what we do is limited by our judgment of people, our relationships with people and our ability to communicate to those people. Anything that can improve our ability to predict the behavior and productivity of people before we hire them, or before we put them in untenable positions, is intensely valuable. There are very few businesses which can be run by one person, yet many of us become disillusioned, lose our ability to trust and consequently try to limit ourselves to only those things we personally produce in order to avoid the problems which arise when you enter employees, partners or associates into the equation. This will keep one's income and one's influences limited and ensure little growth. One person is limited to what he or she can personally produce. With this in mind, studying people and learning some guidelines in order to steer clear of certain personality types becomes essential.

In many businesses our personnel dictate our success or failure. They can literally make or break us. A good manager of people will be well loved and looked after by his staff because they trust his judgment. This trust raises morale. It is a funny quirk, but people want their leader to be as infallible as possible, it gives them a sense of security within which they can grow stronger as individuals. If the "infallible" leader is committed to a goal, then they can feel at ease in supporting him. This position has to be earned by the leader or manager; you cannot buy it with a paycheck or a bonus. It is bought only by being trustworthy and usually right. Notice that you do not have to be always right, just *usually*. The respect and trust of your team is one of the most valuable intangible assets that exist.

Once you have your major goal set, and you have your purpose for any business laid out clearly, it is usually your staff who develop and forward its progress. If they become inspired they are invaluable.

To get behind a goal it must be well defined and concisely stated.

Most people who describe themselves as responsible really mean they are dutiful. The difference is immense and it changes everything. Things one does out of duty are often stressful, require discipline and are rarely fun. Most people confuse responsibility with accountability, duty and blame. The last three are absolutely no fun.

A person may say, I feel responsible for my son's behavior. What they really mean is they feel accountable, to blame, and as if they failed in their duty. Often, a person says he or she feels responsible for something, when they actually mean they feel they were irresponsible about it.

So we have several concepts here that are generally muddled up. We use them rather interchangeably and this causes us considerable confusion. We could actually put them on a scale as follows:

Responsibility.
Duty.
Accountability.
Blame.
Guilt.

[1]Responsibility would correlate to the joy of living band, duty to the bland (conservative) band, accountability to the fear band, and blame to the depression band. This is really a scale of responsibility, where responsibility declines and becomes duty, accountability and blame.

Responsibility can be defined as the ability to control.

Duty can be defined as those things that are expected of one.

Accountability can be defined as those things for which one can be required to account.

Blame can be defined as the process of assigning fault.

We all are generally happy when we are in control. When we learned to drive, we were pleased to be in the driver's seat. We were responsible for where the car went; we were in charge. It felt great. Responsibility is pleasurable.

Duty is less so. Duty by in very nature implies that we did not choose it, that it was chosen for us. We are told that certain things are our duties, that in order to be a "good person" we must live up to our obligations. Some of these obligations are hard to define, but many of us go through life trying to live up to a bunch of obligations that we aren't very clear about to begin with. We feel we should do it; we don't want to let the side down. So we go to church because our mother would be embarrassed if we didn't. We give money to charities we don't believe in, because we feel it's expected. We try and comply in every area of our lives.

Accountability is even more harassing. Driven by fear of being held accountable, we do all sorts of things that we certainly wouldn't choose to do. We hold ourselves accountable for those things, such as the behavior of our children even when they are fully grown, that we cannot possibly hope to control. The government holds us accountable for keeping our accounts so that they can tax us. When we our children, our parents hold us account-

---
[1] See Chapter Five "People and Their Moods."

23

able for our report cards. It all adds up to, I have to do this or I will get in trouble.

Blame is a very strange phenomenon. When things go wrong we immediately look for who is at fault. Lacking someone else to blame, we usually blame ourselves. We are really looking for the source of our trouble. It is as if we believe that placing blame somehow solves things. When somebody close to us is prone to faultfinding we find ourselves going to enormous lengths in order to cover our backs, because we are afraid of being blamed. We laugh at the old jingle:

"The man who can laugh when all goes wrong,
Has found someone to blame it on."

But it is rather a hollow laugh.

Guilt follows blame; it is where we go when there's nothing left to blame but ourselves.

Duty, accountability, blame, and guilt are all lower forms of responsibility. They occur when responsibility has failed.

When you find yourself acting out of duty it might be a good idea to examine whose scripts you are running on. By scripts I mean the story each of us writes for our lives. Everyone writes the script for their life; often they try and foist their ideas and ideals on their friends and family. An example of this is a mother writing the script that her daughter will do all the things SHE wanted to do when she was a girl. Bringing the scripts that you have borrowed or accepted without inspecting them into the light of day gives you the opportunity to choose whether or not you really want to do this. If you find yourself doing things because you are afraid you will be held accountable, you might want to examine exactly why you feel that way.

Full responsibility requires power of choice.

Scale of Responsibility

RESPONSIBILITY LEVEL	ATTITUDE	EMOTION
Fully Responsible	I did it.	Joyful
Responsible	I will be glad to do it	Cheerful
Dutiful	I had to do it.	Bland
Accountable	I admit I did it.	Courageous
Blameful	You did it.	Angry
Pretended Responsibility	What is it? If good = I did it, if bad = I was told to do it.	Sneaky
Evasive	I am afraid I might have done it.	Fearful
Irresponsible	I didn't mean to do it. It was an accident.	Self pity
Guilty	I did it and I am sorry.	Depressed
Victim	You did it to me on purpose.	Apathetic.

Note: This chart will be expanded one day when I get around to it.

Exercises for Chapter Three

1. Write 3 examples of people using the word responsible when they really mean irresponsible:

    _____
    _____
    _____
    _____
    _____
    _____
    _____
    _____
    _____
    _____
    _____
    _____
    _____

2. Write three examples of you doing things from duty, note how you feel when you do them:

    _____
    _____
    _____
    _____
    _____
    _____
    _____
    _____
    _____
    _____
    _____
    _____
    _____
    _____

3. Consider ways you could get them done without you doing them and note them down:

    _____
    _____
    _____
    _____
    _____
    _____

_____

_____

_____

4. Write down some examples of things you do from a sense of obligation to some old idea:

_____

_____

_____

_____

_____

_____

_____

_____

_____

5. Decide which ones you really want to do and which ones you don't:

_____

_____

_____

_____

_____

_____

_____

_____

_____

_____

_____

_____

Chapter Four
PRE-REQUISITES FOR SUCCESS

Just as it is necessary to prepare a flowerbed in order for the plants to be healthy and luxuriant, we need to prepare ourselves to be fertile ground for success. Have you ever stopped to think of what it would be like to be rich and famous?

How do you feel about it?

Does it fill you with excitement or with vague foreboding? Or evoke any other emotion?

Can you tolerate the limelight or do you become paralyzed with fright?

Are you at ease with expensively dressed people, or high priced furnishings, or do you prefer old tennies and well worn but comfortable decor?

Can you speak as easily to the presidents of big companies as you can to blue-collar workers?

Are you driven by fear of failing or by the desire to succeed?

Answer these questions honestly, and then evaluate your chances of achieving huge successes. You may find you need to change something and that may not be easy.

Many of us have a rather vague image of suddenly becoming wealthy and powerful with no clear concept of how to get there, and all that it may entail.

What we can HAVE depends on what we will ACCEPT.

Most of us have self-imposed limits which we have not inspected. They are engraved deeply in our make-up, and we do not notice that we have them. They can be frighteningly *right sounding* until we look a little closer.

A friend of mine was saying, "I always have the money I need. I decided that I would and I always do." Very nice, but this limits her to what she *needs* and omits all the things she would simply *like* to have.

The statement: "All that we are is a result of what we have thought" is attributed to Gautama Siddhartha. It is a pretty workable truth. We arrange our lives to fit the decisions we have made about what we will or will not accept. My friend will not accept having less than she needs, but this set her in a pattern of only getting-by and never getting ahead.

I had an old rhyme about the days of the week that I learned as a child. There were certain attributes for a person born on each day. I no longer recall which day was which, but I DO remember that mine was "Works hard for its living." Somehow I adopted the idea. For most of my life the idea haunted me, I worked very hard for my living. I was unable to do the things I wanted to do that were fun and interesting, I never took vacations; I was stuck with it. It seemed so right, so noble, so ME!

I got lots of mileage out of being a workaholic, lots of admiration, praise and a sense of personal worth. I could sneer at those who lived a life of leisure and scoff at those who were born with silver spoons in their mouths. I could hold those who were motivated by money instead of duty in the greatest of contempt. Finally I got really sick of being Saint Enid and decided I wanted a bigger game to play.

As I am sure you can see, that had been an extremely limiting framework on which to base my life. It locked me into a pattern of working with little financial reward, *always* choosing duty above pleasure or personal affairs. I came second, never first. All my choices were made within that limiting framework. All my decisions were simplified by this idea though. I did not have to do much considering because my path was always obvious. That working myself half to death eventually helped nobody, somehow escaped my attention for the longest time.

Success depends on what you can allow yourself to have. If there is something unacceptable to you about wealth and power, it is certain that you will not create it for yourself. In the same way that I constructed the Scale Of Productivity it is possible to make a [1]Scale Of Acceptance.

What we have depends on what we do; what we do depends on what we are being; what we are being depends on what we think we are.

A person who thinks he is a cook will do the things that cooks do, and have the things that cooks have.

A person who thinks that he can be many different things may become a jack-of-all-trades or he may choose a particular "being-ness" that he wishes to wear.

It is impossible to be a star without *being* a star, doing what stars do and having what stars have.

This illustrates the point that what one can be, do and have depends on what one's level of acceptance allows. If you are convinced that you are a blue-collar worker then that is what you will create, and what you do and have will be dictated by your conviction. If it is more important to you to be popular than effective, you are limited to doing those things which do not damage your image, that make people like you, and you are prevented from taking a hard line position when you should really do so. When faced with a situation such as chronic lack of dependability or poor production it will cause enormous amounts of distress and soul searching and many efforts to avoid the issue. You will have to have far too many justifications before taking the steps to correct the situation. By the time you actually DO act, things may well have escalated out of control and become very expensive.

How you see yourself, what you feel you can be, sets up a pattern for life that locks you into a certain lifestyle, into a certain framework. If you see yourself as mediocre, then you will project that image throughout all that you do, and that will dictate all that you can have.

Attitudes come into existence from the ideas one has accepted as true. Big deeds require big, bold attitudes with powerful ideas fueling them.

Many people have huge ideas, but lack the attitude and will to make them happen. Often there is much talking and planning that occurs but to no result. They have failed to notice that they have limiting ideas already in place. Ideas that prevent funding, or which need technology that does not currently exist, are common with such people. They really know in their

---

[1]See Scale of Acceptance at the end of this Chapter.

31

heart that they will not carry out these grandiose plans. These people cannot actually be what they need to be to make their dreams manifest because they have old ideas which are set in granite and which prevent action.

I have known so many people with big dreams and small will. Will is the "make it happen" factor. Once the goals are set and the ideas in place, it takes will to carry them through to the real world and make things happen.

So the major internal pre-requisites for success are:

1. Having a purpose in which one believes.
2. Setting goals that align with that purpose.
3. Wanting to achieve them.
4. Knowing one can achieve it.
5. Intending to achieve it.
6. Being willing to persevere until one does achieve it.
7. Being willing to continuously adjust ones' ideas and thoughts.

This sets the stage, and lays the foundation for personal success.

SCALE OF ACCEPTANCE

ATTITUDE	REACH	POSSESSIONS	CONDITION
Joy of Living. Abundance. Generosity.	Expansive. "We can have anything we want"	Can have many things. Lots to choose from.	Excellent. Well maintained.
Enthusiasm Prosperity. Shares	Strong ability to reach. "I can have anything I want"	Enjoys toys	Well kept.
Interested Shares some things.	Strong reach in areas of interest. "I can have the things relating to my interests"	Useful and fascinating objects.	Takes great care of the things he finds useful. Other possessions show neglect
Careful Scarcities. Conservative Shares cautiously.	Reaches for things that strengthen security. "We must have insurance"	Stocks up in case of shortages or price increases. Saves things that might come in useful someday.	Excessive care to make things last a long time. Old but in great shape.
Disinterested Shares little, doesn't think of it often	Sporadic reach for things he hopes will be interesting "Maybe this will motivate me."	Has stuff lying around in which he quickly lost interest.	Shows signs of neglect.
Aggressive Shares what he thinks you need with no regard for whether you agree.	Powerful reach for what he wants. "I have to have it. Nothing will stop me"	Guns, fast cars, motor cycles, knives, other weapons. Other possessions are not appreciated.	Either aggressively spotless or utterly neglected.
Pained Shares pain.	Reaches for pacifiers. "I need a drink."	Cabinets full of remedies.	Maintains things only when they break.
Rage Rejects everything	Reaches to destroy. "Who needs it?"	Broken objects and implements of destruction.	Rundown, broken down and dirty.
Hateful Hates everything..	Reaches to reject. "I have it and I hate it."	Spartan. Throws out anything not in use.	Few possessions ruthlessly maintained.
Hidden Rage Shares only things that might hurt you	Reaches to take. "You owe me."	Many objects that are not really owned.	Cluttered.
Pretender Pretends to share.	Reaches to deceive. "My other car is a Rolls."	Collects things that can be made to appear expensive.	Dressed up to look better than it is.
Anxious/Fearful There is not enough to share.	Reaches nervously. "I might lose what little I have."	Few possessions other than bare necessities.	Shabby. Neglected.
Bitterness/Regret There is no sharing.	Does not reach much. "I HAD it and lost it."	Few possessions other than bare necessities.	Shabby. Neglected.
Depressed. They took it all.	No reach. "It is all gone."	Bare necessities	Shabby. Neglected.

Exercises for Chapter Four

1. Look over the Scale of Acceptance carefully and jot down examples of people you know or have known that fit each level:

    _____
    _____
    _____
    _____
    _____
    _____
    _____
    _____
    _____
    _____
    _____
    _____
    _____
    _____
    _____
    _____
    _____
    _____
    _____

2. Examine what type of work would fit each of the persons you listed:

    _____
    _____
    _____
    _____
    _____
    _____
    _____
    _____
    _____
    _____
    _____
    _____
    _____
    _____
    _____
    _____
    _____

_____

3.   Take the 7 internal prerequisites for success and think of people
       who were successful and note where they fit or don't:

_____
_____
_____
_____
_____
_____
_____
_____
_____
_____
_____

4.   Compare your own attitudes to the 7 internal prerequisites:

_____
_____
_____
_____
_____
_____

5.   What would you have to change?

_____
_____
_____
_____
_____
_____
_____
_____
_____

Chapter Five
PEOPLE AND THEIR MOODS

In the two scales (The Chart of Productive Energy and the Scale of Acceptance) you have probably noticed that the first column is the attitude and that the other columns depend on this. This is because what we create for ourselves often arises from our attitudes. These attitudes stem from moods that have become chronic.

There are the daily fluctuations of emotion that we all have, but then there are the *underlying* moods that color our existence. These moods can be charted in a scale from heavy to light. They run under the surface like an operating system in a computer. They are not immediately accessible to us yet they are influencing everything we think and do, every decision we make, everyday of our lives.

This is probably worth further explanation. Much of what we manifest comes from the underlying mood. For example we tell ourselves we are not going to think depressing thoughts or thoughts of possible failure and then we find ourselves doing it anyway. Quickly we mentally change the subject. Later we find ourselves doing it again. Our underlying mood is affecting our conscious decisions.

Something good happens and we temporarily have a lift in mood, we feel happy. Later we sag back to our chronic mood. We tell ourselves we shouldn't feel that way. We give ourselves pep talks or go to a seminar to raise our spirits. It works for a while. Inevitably though we sag back into our mood rut. The reason for this is that we have not reached the cause of the chronic underlying mood and dealt with it.

So, there is <u>surface</u> emotion or mood and chronic mood. Every person that I have worked with has these. Here I am speaking of chronic mood.

Enid Vien

First I am going to divide these moods into broad bands. As we descend the bands the moods get heavier, denser and harder to change or penetrate.

1. The Happiness Band
2. The Bland Band
3. The Aggression Band
4. The Pretense Band
5. The Fearful Band
6. The Depression Band
7. The Illusion Band (neurotic)
8. The Delusory Band (psychotic)

We are only going to concern ourselves with bands one through six. Within each band is a whole spectrum of chronic moods that underlie the daily emotional fluctuations. From these moods we create our attitudes. So the moods actually permeate our entire existence.

We usually only notice a mood when it is intense and do not notice our chronic mood because it is always that way. It is comparable to a mild headache that we only notice when it intensifies or goes away entirely.

MOOD CHART

THE HAPPINESS BAND	Joy of Living Amusement Enthusiasm Cheerfulness Courage Interest
BLAND BAND	Contentment Comfortable Disinterested Boredom Monotony

AGGRESSION BAND	Annoyance
	Irritability
	Hostility
	Belligerence
	Outrage
	Anger
	Fury
PRETENSE BAND	Resentment
	Contempt
	Envy
	Greed
	Jealousy
	Seething but hidden hatred
	Bitterness
	Vengefulness
	Loneliness
	Alienation
	Distrust
THE FEARFUL BAND	Timidity
	Nervousness
	Anxiety
	Dread
	Fear
	Terror
	Fright
	Horror
	Dismay
THE DEPRESSION BAND	Sorrow
	Disgust
	Sadness
	Remorse
	Grief
	Despair
	Apathy
	Failure

People in the upper bands are likely to succeed at whatever they set out to do because such people endow everything with which they come in contact with a happy, productive, light energy. Others respond to this energy and enjoy the emotional lift that they experience in their presence. This makes the upper band person get a lot of support and assistance.

Those least likely to succeed are in the **Depression Band**, for their energy is dense, harder to move and heavier. It is not that the person who is chronically cheerful cannot feel the lower moods, he feels them intensely but he bounces back quickly and does not stick there, whereas the person in the Depression band cannot really *feel* the moods above his level.

Tell a person in the **Depression Band** that he has just won a million dollars and he will rise up a bit, he will come up to worrying about taxes, he has risen to the fear band. His attitude will still be a bit sour, "Why didn't they give it to me in un-taxable funds?" "Well, everyone will be after my money now, I had better hire a bodyguard."

Every win is negated or deflated with a down side. Such persons both expect and dread disappointment.

There is always a cloud of heavy energy around and above these people. I call it the wet blanket effect. If you wish to hear all the reasons you are going to fail just ask one of these chaps; he will be more than happy to oblige.

In the **Fear Band** the person's energy is all d evoted to staying out of trouble, protecting and defending his property, position and rights. This makes his creative focus very narrow and new ideas are likely to be seen as potentially dangerous. He takes action very cautiously. He is unwilling to take even the controlled risk and he panics easily. He is thrifty and spends money very cautiously. He *will* spend money on burglar alarms and have tons of insurance policies. He may have a gun collection and a ferocious dog. His energy feels nervous and he fidgets a lot. He is an alarmist, and potential dangers are often exaggerated which alarms those around him too.

In the **Pretense Band** the individual will prefer to take risks with *your* money and assets. Individuals in this band are caught between fear and aggression so they can be quite destructive as long as they are fairly sure they will not get caught. They are afraid of direct confrontation and terrified of looking bad.

Quite often the pretender will stir up trouble between other people and sit back smugly once the fight begins. As long as they are fighting each other he feels he is safe from discovery or attack. He is a menace in any organization because he is so good at camouflage. He leaves a swath of destruction in his wake.

Pretenders often try and position themselves close to a power source. They then often attempt to make themselves seem indispensable.

The power this gives them is *always* abused.

In the **Aggression Band** the individual is still somewhat driven by fear, he will take some risks but usually they have to contain some very solid, tangible assets or they are a bit unreal to him. Land and real estate are nice and solid and will be the most comfortable for him to reach out and get. He will especially like " fixers" where he has to roll up his sleeves and attack the project physically. Where the aggression is suppressed the person will find physical work a tremendously satisfying and rewarding outlet for his energies. You will find him quite inflexible and resistive to ideas that do not involve huge amounts of physical effort. If you want a physical worker, he is your guy.

In the **Bland Band** the individual will only do things or make investments that fall within his comfort zone. He or she will only do those things that come easily and contain just enough risks to be interesting but not enough to be scary. At this level there's ample free Dynamis, enough to make the person successful enough to maintain a certain comfort level that he will defend as needed. Comfort and predictability are his motivating factors and he will seek out safe, solid investments with minimum risk involved. He loves mutual funds and CDs. He always has a cash cushion and likes to save for a rainy day.

In the **Happiness Band** life has become a game that can be played from many positions, the individual has much more free energy and can reach out much further if he chooses. When the person in this band is a high Dynamis producer he can really make the world his oyster. He is flexible and innovative and he learns easily. He can rebound from losses quickly; he always has a new enthusiasm to cheer him up. His energy is light and his happiness is infectious. He can seem capricious to those in the lower band who watch his mercurial progress through life; they are a bit envious because they do not seem to have his luck, they think. It really isn't luck; it is personal magic. The magic that is really intrinsic to us all.

These cheery souls make the world go round and, if they are ambitious, they will go far. They make life fun without shirking responsibility.

Exercises for Chapter Five

1. Give an example (someone you know) for each of the bands:

   _____
   _____
   _____
   _____
   _____
   _____
   _____
   _____
   _____
   _____
   _____
   _____
   _____
   _____
   _____
   _____

2. Examine successful people you know or know of and place them in
   their band:

   _____
   _____
   _____
   _____
   _____
   _____
   _____
   _____
   _____
   _____
   _____
   _____
   _____
   _____

3. If you have employees or business associates place them in their bands:

    _____
    _____
    _____
    _____
    _____
    _____
    _____
    _____
    _____
    _____
    _____
    _____
    _____
    _____
    _____
    _____
    _____

4. Examine your own attitudes and habits to see which band you fall into:

    _____
    _____
    _____
    _____
    _____
    _____
    _____
    _____

    (Note: There can be some leakage into other close-by bands)

Chapter Six
COMMUNICATION

Big ideas cannot usually be accomplished alone; it takes teamwork and co-ordination. As soon as an idea gets rolling and other people enter the picture, communication becomes of paramount importance.

Poor communication can tear your dreams apart faster than any other factor short of an earthquake. Good, concise, clear communication is the vehicle to achieve the co-ordination and teamwork you will need.

In order for a team to become a functioning unit, certain key ideas must be clearly stated and understood. The most important of these is the purpose of the project and how it aligns with the overall purpose of the company or group. It is the manager's task to express these purposes and get them understood. So if the manager is someone other than yourself, it is your job to make sure *he* understands the purposes and has no confused ideas of his own. The last thing you need is confusion of purpose tarnishing your Golden Nugget.

You are the goal-setter, the originator of the dream. Your team will be as effective as they can align to that dream.

I want to make a distinction here between goals and purposes.

A goal is what you want to do.
A purpose is why you want to do it.

Purposes are broad and general; goals are very specific. A clear statement of your purpose or that of the organization makes it easier to see which goals align with the purpose and which do not.

Whenever one is working with purposes and goals one is working in an area loaded with spiritual and emotional energy. So, I think it is best we take a look at them.

A purpose is a broad general idea. To love broadly, to help, to do good works, to create good effects, are a few examples.

Goals generally stem from purposes. Goals naturally dovetail into the broad general purposes of a being. When they do not and one is working on someone else's purpose or some false purpose the goals do not align with the being's natural state.

A dream is a goal one is not sure one can attain.

Intention or will is the vehicle to make one's goals happen.

A desire is something one wants but does not necessarily seek to achieve.

Sovereign desire is senior to all except the basic purpose of the being. The basic purpose of the being dictates the sovereign desires. These are very powerful and when contacted and intended they seem to be able to shift the very fabric of the universe.

Things you do which are aligned with your basic purpose feel good and right and flow easily. Things you do which are mis-aligned flow with great difficulty.

Most people do not really know their basic purpose, they have traveled a long way from it and have committed many violations of their integrity when their basic purpose has been opposed or thwarted in some way.

Each individual has his own goals and hopes for increased standards of survival. These personal hopes and wishes must not be too far out of alignment with the overall group purpose. If they are too far mis-aligned, the person will be unable to function as an adequate team member and will certainly never become self-motivated or show any useful initiative. Even those who are naturally helpful can become destructive accidentally if they misunderstand the purpose of the group as a whole.

Let us take a simple example: You have a business repairing lawn mowers. Your purpose is to serve your customers well by doing the best job in town so that you keep your customers and can charge a fair price. You hire a manager who thinks the purpose is: To make money. He tolerates shoddy work and rushes the workers to complete the tasks in less time than the jobs should really take, in order to get the jobs out and cash in. At first you are delighted when he proudly shows you the cash receipts. Eventually your business drops off because you lose your most valuable intangible: customer trust.

In our example you had a well-meaning manager who simply did not understand your company's purpose and was following a misconception of his own. When you have a large team, imagine that type of misconception multiplying down the line. You set out to build nuclear reactors and end up with pink bunnies.

This is very annoying and frustrating and in a fit of intense irritation you fire the manager. Muttering about shortsighted managers, you fail to notice that your problem was entirely caused by your failure to clearly delineate and state the company's purpose and to communicate it adequately at the onset.

So, it is the leader's task to make a clear statement of the purpose of the group, and to ensure his managers understand it thoroughly.

It is then the manager's task to communicate it on down the line without altering it or confusing the issue by adding to it.

This is the primary and most vital communication within any group of any kind.

Once this is done, all subsidiary projects and programs can be set-up so that they align to the overall major worthwhile purpose. When a project or program goes haywire one can then immediately examine it to see if it was following this law. If it is found to be "off-purpose," it can then be corrected or scrapped. The key to correction here is in aligning the sub products, projects and programs to the major purpose.

There are some individuals that you may encounter who are chronically "off-purpose." If they are supposed to be filing the receipts, you will find them filing their nails. If they are supposed to be planning the month in advance, you will find them planning the office party instead. These individuals are either unclear as to what the purpose actually IS, or they are suffering from the dread malady I call [1]"A to P to Q." No amount of communica-

---

[1]**A to P to Q**: This is an inability to focus on and complete the task at hand. It is also an inability to think in sequences of actions. For a manager who has spotted a person suffering from this ailment, my advice is to act fast to remove this person from any sensitive position. On any job, position, post or task, the first requirement is

tion, no matter how concise, clear and perfectly expressed, will make a dent in this malady.

However, for most people a well-written or spoken statement of purpose is very helpful and it allows them to either align their own purposes to it, or see that they cannot do so. Once you have a statement well expressed it is good to post it on the wall and refer to it often, this keeps the attention focused, and reminds you and your team exactly what you are working towards.

All products should align with the overall purpose. If you stray too far from this, you will find yourself in a constant state of stress. For example if your expertise is in machinery and you attempt to branch out into haberdashery, you are likely to become too spread out mentally. However if you branch out into a related area such as oils to lubricate the machinery the two products will dovetail and your attention will be less dispersed. The two areas enhance each other. The know-how from one area relates easily to the other.

So we get a rule: All persons on a project and all projects and departments must align to the overall major purpose of the organization. Each project has its goals, when they are not compatible with the overall purpose of the organization they are distracting, time consuming and destructive of the internal harmony that every organism or organization must have to survive. In nature an organism dies when it's internal harmony is compromised beyond a certain point. So does an organization. It follows the laws of nature.

Communication has various vectors, that is to say directions in which it flows. Any organization has internal and external vectors. Internally the communication can be a tangle of threads or it can flow in an organized pattern. This allows the communications to the external world to flow out in an understandable and uniform manner, keeping your customers happy and your staff feeling competent.

Every organization needs a pattern so that communications arrive at the correct person. The correct person being the one whose job description requires him or her to service or otherwise handle that communication. Where you do not have a known and orderly pattern, you have everyone handling everything, or everyone thinking someone else is handling the very things he *should* be handling. The resulting chaos is most alarming!

---

that the person be THERE, not ELSEWHERE. Only when a live person is *actually there* paying attention can any communication be received or sent.

Every position in an organization needs a specific job description that contains its specific duties. Each person needs to know to whom he is answerable, and who answers to him. This seems simple when the organization is small, but as it grows and new personnel are added, it gets more and more complex.

If you have ever walked into a store and tried to do something like get an old printer repaired or something else for which the staff is unprepared, you will immediately see that people naturally do those things they know how to do, and ignore those things that do not fit into the pattern that is familiar and easy. If you are the manager of such a store, you will rapidly find you have no time to manage, because you become the port of last call to which all these oddball items flow. If you are smart, you will rapidly assign someone to handling the communications and routing the tasks to appropriate places.

Every organization, no matter how large or small needs a flow chart that illustrates the most natural and effective way to handle its daily traffic. Once this is done it is easy to show new staff and old the chart. Many people work better when they can see the pattern.

Let us take, for example, a factory that manufactures pencils, it has to have several distinct departments. They would break down to: Personnel, Marketing, Sales, Accounting, Supply, Production, Complaints, Quality Control and Co-ordination of all of these. Within each department there are several functions, all of which must align to the final product: A high quality pencil in the hands of a satisfied customer.

When you really examine it, the amount of functions is pretty amazing. If any one function is missing or out of synch, the entire organization eventually crumbles. This does not even begin to list the management functions, such as new product line planning, re-tooling or financial planning. So we see that even what appears to be a simple operation becomes complex when we are looking at an organization. Each facet here must align to the major product: "A high quality pencil in the hands of a satisfied customer." Yet each of the facets has to have a communication channel to certain other facets in order to operate smoothly.

I have drawn out a very sketchy sample to give you a feel for this concept.

Enid Vien

A SAMPLE ORGANIZATION (Pencil Factory.)

Management Strata

Person-nel	Marketing	Sales	Accounts	Supply	Production	Complaints	Quality Control
Hiring	*Advertis-ing*	*Orders*	*Payroll*	*Purchas-ing*	*Manufac-ture*	*Correc-tions*	*Safety*
Training	*Promotion*	*Cus-tomer Service*	*Billing*	*Inventory*	*Packaging*		*Inspec-tions*
Records	*Package design*	*Ship-ping*	*Payables*	*Supply inspect*	*Product Inventory*		
Disci-pline		*Outside Reps.*	*Taxes/Insu-rance*		*Machine Upkeep*		

SAMPLE FLOW CHART

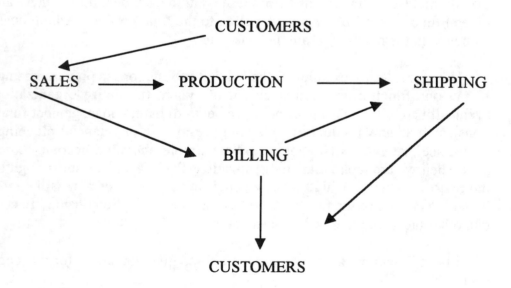

50

The flow chart illustrates the flow of communication for a routine incoming order. Every organization has its own pattern which, when laid out on paper, gives it a structure of channels on which communications can flow. The factory would have another flow chart for incoming supplies, for incoming bills, for quality control, and complaints. The personnel in each area need to know the flow patterns for their particular duties in order for the communications to arrive at their appropriate destinations. This may seem abysmally obvious to you, but I assure you it is *not* obvious to new, or at times even old, personnel. I have done flow charts for several large corporations that had no clue as to what was happening to their vital data flows.

My husband took a little ink jet printer into a computer store for repairs, they called and said it needed an expensive part, which would cost more than the printer was worth and they required $40.00 for just looking at the machine. We happened to know where we could get the part so he went to get it back.

On arrival at the store he was kept waiting for over an hour and had a chance to watch the operation. Quite a crowd of irritated people was collecting in the doorway blocking both incoming and outgoing traffic. They were irritated because they were just left to wait. No one came to explain why the delay. In fact, they were pretty much ignored after the initial "Can I help you?"

After an hour David decided he had spent enough time "watching the operation" and went in search of a manager to whom he explained his situation. The manager disappeared into the back room and did not reappear for another fifteen minutes. When he emerged his face was red. "We have fifty machines just like yours back there, and none of them are labeled." He said. "I will waive the $40.00 fee, and when we find it I will personally send it to you."

Two weeks later the machine arrived. Lo and Behold! It has worked perfectly ever since. I can only assume that it was not our machine, but one of the other unlabelled printers in the infamous back room. So, what happened to our machine, and did some luckless Wight end up with that lemon?

This was a MAJOR chain store, I predicted that they would not be around for long, and recently I heard that they had closed their doors. They were suffering from a lack of flow charts. This was clogging their communication channels to their customers, even to the point of traffic jams in their doorway. The inertia of big corporations and the inability of the owners to see the actual balance sheets probably made them appear to survive for some time after they were actually insolvent. It is easy to predict that insolvency follows inefficiency, but less easy to perceive exactly what is causing the inefficiency.

Most inefficiency is a direct result of communication breakdowns. These breakdowns usually occur due to unknown flow patterns, added inapplicable patterns, or omitted steps along the way. When you have a flow chart it is much easier to trace the communication breakdowns to their source point.

HOW TO MAKE A FLOW CHART

1. You pretend you are an order for a product.
2. Walk yourself physically through all the steps the order must go through in order to arrive at the end of the line as a filled order.
3. As you do this, note down each step and department that is involved, in the correct sequence.
4. Once this is done, have someone else go through the same steps and compare the two.
5. Draw it out on a large piece of paper with arrows.

Each person should have a chart for his own area to which he or she can refer. This is especially important for anyone who is handling the channels of communication to and from your public. Knowing how things work and the channels on which they flow, is extremely empowering to the individual. It enables him to see how he contributes to the teamwork of the organization as a whole. It gives him a sense of security, as well as one of belonging. Security comes from knowing the score, from knowing what is going on, and knowing what is expected of one. This is an important thing to know about employees for the psychology of an employee is different from that of an entrepreneur or business owner.

It is the nature of a businessman or entrepreneur to deal with risk, controlled risk, but nevertheless risk. It is the nature of an employee to seek security and avoid risk. The clever businessman takes the risks while providing the safe haven that gives his employees the sense of shelter that they crave. It is useless to expect your employees to be like you. If they were, they would be business owners too.

Exercises for Chapter Six

1. Explain the distinction between a purpose and a goal:

    _____
    _____
    _____
    _____
    _____
    _____
    _____
    _____
    _____
    _____
    _____
    _____

2. Draw a diagram showing what happens when the flow of business is impeded:

3. Draw a flow chart for some business with which you are familiar and notice where it should flow more smoothly if it not going well:

Chapter Seven
LEADERSHIP

Thousands of words have been written on this subject. Amusingly enough, usually by people who have not been in leadership positions.

As the twenty-first century inexorably begins, it is interesting to ponder about the type of leaders that will emerge in the next millennium and to speculate on the necessities that will differ from the centuries gone by, and on the demands that the Age of Knowledge will require.

The idea that some people are natural leaders and that we can study them and copy what they do or do not do, seems a natural enough method for wannabe leaders to utilize. We humans are wonderful mimics and many of our learning patterns are deeply rooted in our innate talent for mimicry.

Whether or not the study of leaders has ever helped anyone *become* one is unclear to me. I have run large organizations and sections of large organizations with some success, yet I would not classify myself as the leadership type. I have, however, learned to be passable in that department. So I am living proof that *some* things about leadership can be learned.

I am about to embark on an attempt to define the qualities that a leader must have in order to succeed.

Firstly, a leader must inspire people to follow him. What is it that inspires such trust?

POISE. The person must have self-confidence and self-possession.

FOCUS. He must appear to know where he is going and what he is doing.

WILL. He must have the drive and enthusiasm for the accomplishment of the group goals.

COMMUNICATION. He must be able to skillfully communicate with conviction the programs that align to the overall thrust of the organization.

INTEGRITY. He must command respect in his personal behavior and business dealings.

COMPETENCE. He must be able to demonstrate the ability to do things as well as or better than his followers.

These six qualities are essential for any leader. These alone will get one by. They will not guarantee that you become president, but they will ensure that you command respect.

There are leaders and then there are Great Leaders. The second category is in an entirely separate class.

What is it that makes a Great Leader like Gandhi, Elizabeth the First, Jesus or even those like Hitler, Stalin or Alexander the Great?

Can we find common denominators for all great leaders, whether they appear politically correct today to us today or not?

Whether they lead by the pen or the sword one thing is very clear; all of these people had an unusually large quantity of life energy. They seem larger than life and their accomplishments are well beyond the ordinary. All the leaders mentioned above led vast numbers of people, some by right of conquest, some by birth and some because the people acclaimed them.

So we have the following categories:

1. Right of Conquest
2. Inherited Position
3. Business Success
4. Popular vote or acclaim.

EXAMPLES OF POWERFUL PEOPLE BY CATEGORY

Right of Conquest	Genghis Khan	Alexander	Napoleon
Inherited Position	Elizabeth 1	Queen Victoria	Richard Lion heart
Business Success	Henry Ford Lee Iacocca Werner Erhard	Tony Robbins Mary Kay Ash Coco Chanel	Ross Perot John Sculley (Apple)
Popular Vote or Acclaim	Gandhi Jesus Churchill G. Washington Hitler	Martin Luther King Buddha President Kennedy	Billy Graham Margaret Thatcher President Clinton

Today it is hard for us to accept that Hitler would fall in the last category, elected by popular vote, yet it is sadly true. He captured the attention and was able to lead an enthusiastic Germany to disaster, because he had the gift of oratory. He was believable and he could whip up the emotions of the common man by using his gift. This illustrates clearly that rule by popularity eventually falls down, because often people elect those rascals who say what they, the voters, want to hear and who make promises which they cannot keep, in order to get those almighty votes.

I have tried here to put only people who are generally well known. It is noteworthy that there is less and less in the first two categories in the modern world, leaving us with Business Leaders and Popular Vote or Acclaim as the two which we are most concerned with today. I have omitted the category of scientific and educational leaders because they are not visibly leading, the knowledge trickles down to us, but no one actively follows an Einstein or a Bertrand Russell. They stand beside society and influence its direction of thought, but they do not lead us en masse to do battle with higher mathematics or logical analysis. Their products have a long-term effect but as modified by political or business leaders.

So, what do all these extraordinary people share as qualities? Why do or did people follow them, even in some cases to the point of self-destructive madness?

In all of those that are my contemporaries and of whom I have some personal observation, it is noteworthy that they can all speak very well and with enormous conviction. They can command an audience. Every one of them has the star quality that in the theater is called stage presence. They seem more *present* than the ordinary individual. While their message is important, the same words when spoken by someone else do not have the same effect. We are feeling the impact of life force. The sheer force of character communicates to us along with the speech and willy-nilly we are swept along in the current.

I conclude that we are looking at individuals with tremendous amounts of Dynamis: life energy.

Their life energy is so powerful that it influences and increases the energy of those within their reach. If we postulate that it is this life energy that enlivens and animates our bodies then these individuals have so much of it that it can spill over and add to that of others.

This gives us our first ingredient: An unusually high amount of Dynamis being emanated along with the communication spoken, or even written.

The next thing I notice is that each one is able to direct their focus with intensity when speaking. Along with the extra quantity of life energy comes high volume and extremely powerful amounts of will. The will to do whatever it is they are doing or espousing is very strong in these people.

Charm, or charisma seems to be rather over-rated; some of these people were not charming in the slightest degree, yet they commanded attention. People listened to them. Most of them were not persuasive or even particularly skilled at debate, few were even diplomatic, but they were all passionately sold on their various agendas. However, when charisma is also present such a person is pretty much unstoppable.

So we get our second and third ingredients: ~~will and passion.~~ I have been unable to isolate any other qualities they all appear to share. Some empower people, some do not, some are selfless, and some are not. The key ingredient is the terrific quantity of life force.

There are three important questions that I asked myself:

1. Why does one person seem to have more than his or her fair share of life force?
2. Are we equal in potential? Or not?
3. Can one beef up his volume of Dynamis?

These are questions that have baffled philosophers for a long, long, time.

Even Doctors get into this puzzle, why does one patient survive against all odds, and another simply lie down and die?

How come one person can be so passionate, so involved, so purposeful, and another can barely decide what to have for lunch?

Why are children within the same family and experiencing the same environment so frequently quite different in their psychology?

My Dynamis Theory makes some sense out of the above tangle. Each of us is, in our own way a creator. We are generating our own Dynamis. Whether there is a higher power to which we are connected generating limitless potentials I will leave to the theologians for the moment.

Some people naturally generate more energy than others. Most of us ALSO have impediments to our energy creation plus old unwanted energy of various types that we lug around with us like old junk we hope will be useful someday.

It is unlikely that we each started off with the same capacity and volume, since each of us is a unique blend of qualities. Just as kittens in a litter vary in strength, so do we. Even so, a weaker individual operating at full capacity is undoubtedly much more powerful than one operating in the condition we normally see here on Earth.

So let us start by not expecting to all be alike. Not only would this be boring but it would ruin most of our games. Every chess game would end in a stalemate, and every competition result in a draw. Boring!

59

Enid Vien

Individuals have certain qualities and these are blended any number of ways.

First we have **general volume of Dynamis production**. While this can fluctuate, it has a normal volume for each individual.

Next we have **intellect** that we use to make sense out of intuition, imagination, hunches and data, in order to direct our efforts.

Next we have **will**, the engine that we use to move whatever mountain is currently misbehaving.

Other than volume of Dynamis production, all the above are different types of thought. The qualities give us a formula:

Dynamis Volume + Intelligence + Will + Imagination + Intuition = Individual Impact on Society.

Where any one of these is out of balance, high or low, the individual is stronger or weaker in that area, giving us the wild variety of personalities we see around us.

A high volume, high intellect, strong willed, imaginative and intuitive person will tend to rise to the top of whatever profession or area of endeavor he chooses.

A high volume, low intellect, high will, low imagination and little intuition person will probably do very well in areas where sheer power can prevail and is important. The heroes of the Wild West mostly fall in this category.

However, even with all these qualities present, success is unlikely unless there is focus and the ability to express the dreams to others in such a way that they will get behind the wagon and push.

A person without a dream is a person who has given up on life. Our hopes and desires give us the will to live, to drive forward, and to reach for the stars.

A great leader is able to align the dreams of others with his own larger dream, thus forming a juggernaut that elevates him into power. The dream has to be large and embracive enough so that the dreams of others can be included in the action. Groups form due to mutual perception of survival principles. They rally around a dream. Whether the dream is of life after death, as in churches, or of financial security, or world peace, is immaterial to this point. All groups have a dream of some sort. The bigger and more embracive the dream, the more other individuals can align to that dream.

A truly great dream can practically revive the dead.

A person can have tremendous personal Dynamis volume, great intellect, intuition and will, but without a dream he has no focus for his talents. He has nowhere to go. With nowhere to go, obviously no one can follow him.

So we get these rules of leadership:

Rule One: Have somewhere to go. (Major purpose.)
Rule Two: State the purpose clearly.
Rule Three: Align all sub goals to the major dream.
Rule Four: Keep the dream alive in the minds of those who follow.

Once these are in place lesser, but still valuable, rules can be helpful.

1. Give positive directions.
2. Always listen to the fellow actually doing the job.
3. Even when you are listening, always look for yourself.
4. Never assume, find out for sure.
5. Delegate power.

This last rule is worth a comment or two. Like love, power isn't power until you give it away. Some people like to keep a very tight rein on all decision-making and tight control over everything that happens in their organization. This is not only exhausting it is self-defeating. It dis-empowers your staff terrifically. If you cannot trust a person to make the decisions relating to his position, get someone in there you *can* empower and trust. A leader who has to descend into the nit-picking daily decision making will not have enough time to keep the broad overall, slightly detached, viewpoint that is necessary in order to lead. This keeps organizations small, limited by how much ONE person can directly control.

Holding all the controls in one spot is rather like attempting to drive several cars at once. In other words, it is impossible.

Empowering other people empowers you!

Exercises for Chapter Seven

1. Add some powerful personalities to my list, putting them in the correct categories:

   _____
   _____
   _____
   _____
   _____
   _____
   _____
   _____
   _____
   _____

2. Write a short essay describing why it is important to learn to delegate:

   _____
   _____
   _____
   _____
   _____
   _____
   _____
   _____
   _____
   _____
   _____
   _____
   _____
   _____
   _____

3. Fill in the blank:

"Empowering others_____"

Chapter Eight
POWER

Power is a very hot word. It is good for conjuring up many visions of tyranny, oppression and subjugation in the minds of many people. So much so that we have the cynical little saying that: "power corrupts and absolute power corrupts absolutely." It doesn't have to be that way. In fact it is the *abuse* of power that stands out as so memorable, while we forget the more gentle and helpful uses to which power can be applied. Like many such apparently wise sayings, it is not always true.

We all use power every day, but we do not always think of it as power. We use electricity and car engines, computers and watches without considering these as uses of power. We use our minds and our abilities in order to direct this power, to decide what we should DO with it.

Personal power comes from within. It is the force we use to drive our desires along the pathways we wish them to travel towards the destinations we have chosen.

The key question here is: What determines the degree of power a person can wield and can it be increased?

Before we can really attack this question it is necessary to really define power.

Power, in business, is the ability to direct motion. This is a very important concept to grasp. Undirected motion produces chaos. Directed motion produces order. Energy, when it is not harnessed, does not travel in predictable pathways. In business or life we require our energy to travel down pathways that have a predictable outcome. The more we can direct the motion of objects and people the more power we generate.

Power and control have a great deal to do with each other. We control the motion of a car and we have power over that car. If we control the car badly, we are likely to collide with some portion of the physical universe and lose that power either temporarily or permanently. It is the same with businesses and with people. If we have power over the direction and motion of many people and we use poor control, then we are on a collision course that will eventually cause us to lose our power.

People allow you to control their direction and motion because they trust you. Violate that trust with bad control and you will not be in power for long.

There is another type of power worthy of mention; this is the power of influence. It is a variation on personal power and it is used in marketing, advertising, public relations and sales. Some people are very talented at influencing others; they are usually good with words and can channel their emotions into focused patterns that captivate attention from an audience. Words have no power of their own, but over time we have loaded them with our mental energy so today certain words communicate terrific power when written and even more when spoken with conviction.

When you make plans and give orders you are using control, which generates power. This is easily seen in martial arts where the motion of the adversary is used by adding to it. You pull or push the person in the direction he is already going, thus producing much more power than you could if you simply blocked his motion. Organizations can use this same principle. You direct the flows more exactly in the direction where they would naturally flow. This takes MUCH less effort than trying to redirect the stream uphill. Then you remove barriers and impediments from the path of those who work and produce, which gives them a clear pathway to go forward. This is why it is so important to work with people whose goals align with that of the organization. They are going in a direction that is not unnatural to them. Therefore, to generate power you have to have a workable understanding of control. Control is a simple subject that can appear very complex when you need to control large numbers of people and products.

Production involves motion. Every motion has a beginning, middle, and an end. It has a start, a change of position and a stop. Motions also have direction. Within the larger motion of production, are many smaller motions that add up to a completed product. Each of these motions must align with the overall direction. Undirected motion produces chaos; directed motion produces order.

Control becomes very unpopular when it is badly used. Good control *feels* good. There are many ways to mess control up; the direction is incorrect for the desired product or there is something wrong with the start, the middle or the end. An example of something wrong with the "start" segment, is when you give someone a task to perform and while he is attempting to do it, you pull him off it and give him something else to do, then something else. He now has three tasks started and nothing finished. This is very disconcerting for him and he starts to feel pressured and overwhelmed. Managers who do this consistently break down their employees' confidence and make them feel unfulfilled, harried and anxious. It actually lowers productivity. Naturally there are times when it is necessary to pull someone off for a more time sensitive job, but it must be done only when really essential.

An example of something wrong with the "change" segment of control would be setting up a flow chart so that the particles being produced have to reverse direction instead of flowing smoothly along to the final product.

An example of something amiss with the "stop" section would be never being satisfied with the product, continuously calling it back for revisions and corrections so that it is never finished. Also one could stop it too soon, before it is up to the standards that are really needed.

Every communication, every action and every m   otion has its proper span of start change and stop, along with appropriate direction and velocity. This also applies to one's entire life. I call this the action span. Each set of "start-change-end" is one action span. There can be action spans within action spans. The whole concept of production-line factories is based on this idea. It is also necessary to examine this in terms of the productivity within an office or any business.

The speed and direction of these action spans is also vitally important. A line that moves too slowly, too quickly or in fitful spurts will damage the ability to predict the quantity of the end product. Making too many of the wrong items can be extremely wasteful.

So, the answer to one of the questions I originally posed in this chapter: what determines the degree of power a person can wield and can it be increased, lies partly in the application of intelligence to direct force. There are two types of power, that which one has natively (internal), and that over which one has control (external). External would include cars, organizations, employees and so on. One directs and aligns the power of external factors.

How much personal (internal) power any individual has depends on two main factors. How much life energy (Dynamis) he natively has, and how much of this energy is dammed up within himself and unavailable for his use.

We are not all born with equal amounts of Dynamis available to us. It is obvious from very young that some of us are far more dynamic, vibrant and full of life than others. It seems that the start of this lifetime is not necessarily a Tabula Rasa (clean slate). However, it is what we have to work with.

At birth we have the Dynamis with which we are going to approach life. As we travel through life, events happen which teach us some very bad lessons. Events that teach us to draw back from life itself are the worst of these. Painful and shocking traumas both physical and emotional are common during childhood and puberty. The more Dynamis a person has available, the better able he is to weather these storms. Along with these growing pains comes the indoctrination into whatever belief system prevails in his family, his school and often his religion. Generally in our culture, the boys are conditioned to ignore pain and conceal their emotions, while the girls are taught to get their own way through manipulating the emotions the men are pretending they do not have.

Let us take an individual with average Dynamis production. He has survived the birth trauma and is beginning to learn the use of his body and mind. Crawling around he bumps into objects, then while learning to walk he collects the usual amounts of bumps and bruises. None of this is too much to overcome and he remains cheerful, open and is still reaching for new experience. Then, for the first time, he is left with a baby-sitter. This is new.

The sitter, busy watching TV, fails to n otice that things are very quiet for quite some time. Long enough for our young adventurer to get in trouble.

Discovering that he can climb up the door and reach the ha   ndle, Tommy lets himself out. Never having negotiated stairs before, he tumbles down the front steps and hits his head on the pavement. Like most head injuries, this gash bleeds profusely. Naturally, he screams at the top of his lungs. The screaming manages to penetrate through the sounds of the television. Panic stricken, the sitter rushes out and grabs him. Seeing all the blood, she rushes him into the house leaving a trail of blood behind them, where his parents are bound to see it, if not step in it. She cleans the gash up and when she sees it is not serious, she absolutely loses her composure. Yelling at full capacity, she proceeds to tell him what a bad, spoiled, naughty brat he is. How could he do this to her? She slaps his chubby legs hard and puts him to bed. She locks him in his room and resumes her important mission in life, watching her TV shows. Sobbing injured and brutalized, our young hero finally falls asleep.

This sleep is rapidly interrupted when his mother, anxious and having been thoroughly frightened by the trail of blood, rushes in and snatches her child from his bed. She also scolds him. From this experience he learns to be more cautious, less adventurous, and he gets the idea that he has to be watched over because he is bad. Life is not quite so interesting after this.

The big day finally comes and he is packed off to kindergarten, abandoned in a room full of children, all of whom seem to know what is going on. It makes him nervous and he looks around for his mother, only to find she is GONE! The other kids tease him for being a crybaby and later for sulking. He learns, you cannot depend on your mother for everything; she may abandon you when you need her most. More importantly, he learns to not reveal his emotions to his peers, who have just taken unfair advantage. Tommy becomes more stoical in his attitude, passively accepting many of the things that come his way.

As time goes on he learns to avoid trouble, to act "normal" and to worry about his health. This is not because he is afraid of getting sick. He is simply afraid of needles, of doctors, dentists and of other mysterious figures all of which seem to be involved in some way with his physical wellbeing. He learns about death and injuries, but no one really sits down and talks to him. He wonders why one of the kids in his class has two missing fingers on his hand. It bothers him. When he tries to speak of it he is rapidly told to hush, "We don't mention other people's peculiarities."

The indoctrination continues with sports, where he is taught to be tough. If you get a bruise, you must not rub it, unless you enjoy being called a sissy. All of this is teaching him to lock up his Dynamis, to appear acceptable and to join in the game of pretending you are fine, when in truth you are hurt.

By the time Tommy discovers that girls are not just wimpy boys, this stoic attitude has become ingrained. His Dynamis is quite inhibited by the stonewall he presents to the world. He eventually falls in love, and then there is one person with whom his guard is down. When she betrays him, his heart turns to ice and the stonewall thickens. He is now eighteen and the scars he has developed and the wall of ice around his heart will dictate the rest of his life. More germane to my topic, the life energy, the Dynamis available to him has an impeded flow. The love and spontaneity he has inhibited is part of his Dynamis, and it is now locked up behind a shell of stoicism. He may be unaware of the shell, he may become aware of it later on and want to be spontaneous, loving and extroverted, but the risk of injury to the sensitive inner core is too great. He just can't take the chance.

Enid Vien

When one's heart is open, the chances of pain are greater, but so are the chances of joy. So Tommy has icy bandages around his heart. He has locked himself into this prison of invisible chains where nothing can reach him, or touch him, for good or ill.

The person who is open to experience can learn and grow. This is as useful in business as it is in relationships. The better you are able to feel the people and the world around you, the less likely you are to make mistakes. All perceptive abilities are valuable tools with which to make judgments and decisions. Shut off a perception and you have to that degree shut off communication and the ability to experience life.

Often the person tries to overcome his reluctance and cautiously tries to love again, but now he has a thought pattern that tells him that reaching out is dangerous. He is likely to bolt like a frightened rabbit if he perceives any chance of betrayal. Sometimes the impression of the past betrayal is so deep that it is all he *can* see, causing him to misinterpret current events and bring about the very thing he most wishes to avoid.

These moments of anguish cut very deeply into a person's soul. I call them Psychic Wounds, and these wounds are one of the things that are tackled and clarified in [1]Clearing.

Psychic Wounds spawn new attitudes that are less productive, more depressed and often illogical. When we are under heavy emotional stress, we think less clearly than under normal circumstances. Our intellectual capacity is colored by strong emotions at these times. We tend to exaggerate and dramatize the emotional pain in our thoughts. This tears down the internal universe we have erected, makes it invalid and wrong. The things that we had considered most right about ourselves become tinted with dark emotion. What we once considered so right has now become utterly wrong. We swing wildly from one extreme to another. (The Pendulum Effect.) We make vows to never be caught with our pants down again. We formulate policies that are designed to catch and eradicate any similar event in the future. We become suspicious, watchful and untrusting. Believing this is serving us we engrave it in our thought patterns, at the same time trying to forget the event from which we arrived at these ideas. We remember the new policies and new attitude to life, though. These we wear like a badge of honor, constant reminders of our fallibility and our vulnerable aspects.

---

[1] **Clearing**: A set of techniques used by a Clearing Practitioner or Coach to alleviate dammed up Dynamis (life force) and allow the individual's natural Dynamis to flow.

It is these thought patterns that create actual patterns of repetitive events in our lives. This is quite maddening. We watch people close to us make the same errors in judgment over and over, we wonder why they never seem to learn. Naturally, it is harder to inspect our own patterns, so we overlook the obvious. These people with repetitive patterns are often reflecting back to us a pattern of our own. We really do have something to do with why they are in our lives.

Exercises for Chapter Eight

1.   Give three examples of psychic wounds:

_____
_____
_____
_____
_____
_____
_____
_____
_____
_____
_____
_____

2.   Write out new policies the person may have adopted due to the wounds:

_____
_____
_____
_____
_____
_____
_____
_____
_____
_____
_____
_____
_____
_____
_____
_____

3.   Examine what effects these policies will be likely to cause:

_____
_____
_____
_____
_____
_____
_____

_____

_____

_____

_____

_____

4. Give three examples of good uses of power:

_____

_____

_____

_____

_____

_____

_____

_____

_____

_____

_____

Chapter Nine
The Game of Life

Every endeavor can be likened to a game. Business, family, marriages, groups of any description, all have a definite arena or sphere in which they occur. This could be called the playing field. Each group has a particular world of its own, one created by the players in the game, they make the rules and set the stage within the sphere. These spheres come into contact with other spheres in the world where the rules and ideas may be very different. This can cause friction when the spheres are too different or can be helpful if the spheres are aligned.

In creating a group of any type it can be valuable to inspect the components of a game. What makes a good and enjoyable game and what makes a game popular and worthwhile is well worth knowing.

Games all have to have playing fields, whether it is a chess board or a football field, a stage, a boardroom or computer screen, all games have a distinct set of boundaries in which they are played.

Within these boundaries the game itself is played.

Games have common denominators, those basics that have to be present for interaction to occur. Once the playing field is set, the parameters of the game itself can be established. We can get very involved in games, very emotional, very serious about them. They can become a focal point for our lives.

Every game has a goal, a direction towards which all the efforts are aimed.

It has purposes.
There are rules.
There are players.
There are opposing players.
There are rivals or competitors.
There are special skills and knowledge.
There are scorekeepers.
There are referees or judges.
There are prizes which attaining the goal brings.

Many games have other games within the game itself. The game of competing for who gets to play what position, the game of choosing the players for a team, the game of changing the rules are just a few that come to mind.

As I said before, every game has its own sphere or arena. In business, the game is usually played within its buildings or workspace. Taking the example of a factory that builds cars, we can form a picture of the world within that factory. People work there and develop skills that are meaningless to those on the outside. They develop special vocabulary to describe the things they do and make. They understand each other within that arena in a way that those who have never worked there cannot. The frame of reference is different. It is the same with a football team. The team members share the frame of reference of the game. It also has its own set of words to describe different plays and its own set of skills and rules. Even a religion or church has its own sphere of reference, its own specialized terms and its own rules and reference points.

The people you work with feel strengthened by having a position within a game wherein they know the rules. Whenever large organizations go through sweeping changes you will see the members of the group became unstabilized, anxious and confused. The faster the changes happen, the more distressed the people become. This is not an argument for not introducing change; it is however, a statement that change must be approached with careful forethought. Wherever possible change should be approached slowly, giving everyone involved a chance to get used to the idea before it is implemented. This minimizes the upsets. When it is necessary to make a sweeping change at once, it should be done swiftly and a program to retrain and deal with the fallout implemented.

You will find the vast bulk of people are not particularly keen on new ideas. They treat them like an alien who has accidentally strayed onto a football field and interrupted the game; they are half frightened, half annoyed. Then there are some who are absolutely opposed to change of any sort. Almost everyone has some reaction to sudden changes. Generally speaking, the originator of every new idea of any breadth and scope has had to fight to get it to be implemented. When the new idea is one that challenges some favorite fixed notions the reactions can be violent and even deadly.

We give ideas power by endowing them with extra force such as religious doctrine stating that you must believe the earth is flat, or the sun revolves around the earth, or that computers are infernal contraptions designed by demons. In business one runs into a similar phenomenon such as the attitude that we've always done it this way. It worked in 1925 so it will work today.

Illogical? Certainly!
Powerful? Indisputably!

Once you run head-on into a mind-set that appears to have been cast in concrete, you have probably already changed things too quickly, and you have certainly failed to present your changes in the most favorable light. Often we think of public relations as an external subject to one's business, but PR is also an internal factor that must be considered.

PR is the art of popularizing a product or program.

This means making it POPULAR. The "Do it my way, or hit the highway." attitude breeds intense discontent and eventual mutiny. It is best to only utilize force of this type in emergency situations. The power of gentle friendly communication is most needed when change is affecting a great many people.

When you have time, it is better by far to survey your personnel individually about your proposed changes, asking questions which are designed to bring out their attitude towards them. This isolates your trouble spots BEFORE they make a major flap at a staff meeting or catch you off guard. It also gives your staff a chance to give you their opinions. From the survey you can tell how much education or re-training has to be done in order to make a smooth transition. You can start a PR campaign to popularize the program; you can adjust the program or even scrap it in some cases. A simple survey can open many doors.

Here is a sample of some survey questions regarding an upcoming change:

1. How do you like the idea of changing our focus to ready wear from designer clothing?
2. What do you like best about it?
3. What do you like least about it?
4. What effect do you think it will have on your department?
5. What effect do you think it will have on your job?
6. Is this an idea you can get behind at the moment?
7. Do you have any ideas that could help smooth the transition?

It is best to have someone uninvolved ask the questions and jot down the answers along with their comments regarding the person's attitude. Then you can read the answers and try and get a feel for the emotional climate of your workplace. This gives you a great deal of data with which to plan your changes.

Exercises for Chapter Nine

1.   What makes staff feel secure?

_____
_____
_____
_____
_____
_____

2.   What does change do to this security?

_____
_____
_____
_____

3.   How do you instigate changes minimizing bad effects?

_____
_____
_____
_____
_____

4.   Write out three examples from your life when you ran into an immovable mindset:

_____
_____
_____
_____
_____
_____
_____
_____
_____
_____

5.   How could you have influenced the outcome to get a better result?

_____
_____
_____

Enid Vien

_____
_____
_____
_____
_____
_____

6.   Fill in the blank: "PR is the art of _____a product or pro-
     gram.

Chapter Ten
CREATING ABUNDANCE

Once you have clearly seen what you would most enjoy doing, then you need to remove all the possible roadblocks to achieving your heart's desire. Sometimes one needs to remove the barriers that are keeping you from seeing what you really want to do. If your dreams are big ones then it becomes necessary to set the stage for their accomplishment. This starts with you. Your old spiritual baggage must be tackled, old wounds brought into the light of day and examined, limiting ideas exhumed and given a decent burial. Your life force, which has been dammed up behind the [1]Psychic Scars left by Psychic Wounds must be cleaned up so it may flow freely once again.

Any considerations you may have regarding deserving success must be looked at, especially those nasty little thoughts you instantly quash before quickly reaffirming your conscious wishes and decisions. Like invisible bacteria these nasty little thoughts breed, darkening your field of Dynamis, making you use energy to suppress them, energy that could have been utilized in forwarding your dreams.

In order to free yourself of any factor that dis-empowers you, you have to look at it. Stuffing these unwelcome thoughts down and thinking positive thoughts simply allows them to fester *underneath* the positive thoughts.

Anything that is not squarely viewed has a nasty tendency to stick around.

If you do not see the dirty dishes, it is certain that you will not wash them. If you refuse to acknowledge the presence of super-charged energy on a subject you will certainly not do well in that area. Not looking at things ties up tremendous amounts of life energy. It is hard to force your attention off the things you do not wish to see. You can prove this to yourself by not thinking of a purple cow with yellow spots. Not as easy as it sounds, is it?

Once an old idea has been thoroughly examined it can vanish from your universe, where it was once a fixture. It is the force of emotion and will that you felt when the idea

---

[1] The reason I keep calling these Psychic Scars and Psychic Wounds is to stress that these are not really mental effects; they are blows to the spirit. One is less spunky; less full of élan vital after one has experienced one of these.

was formulated that holds it in place. So these unsettling thoughts that negate your conscious wishes tend to repeat themselves, popping out of the woodwork of your mind like termites. Once you have captured the thought then you can thoroughly examine it. Where did you get this idea? Was it really someone else's idea? What made you adopt it?

Partially viewing something will release the surface tension.

Fully seeing something *exactly* as it is will cause it to vanish in its current form.

A good exercise to start exorcising one's personal demon thoughts is to write them all down. Especially the silly ones. Exposing them to the light of day can be both amusing and therapeutic. While *intellectually* you know these thoughts are foolish or harmful, *emotionally* they keep slinking into your thoughts until you do examine them.

The thoughts which keep recurring and which you cannot seem to discard, even when you know intellectually they are mental termites, are usually from old Psychic Wounds.

Psychic Wounds are not ordinary memories; they are impressions that scarred you so deeply they became etched in your consciousness. The thoughts that you had at the time have become embedded within the impression. When faced with similar circumstances, a gateway opens to the old impression and the supercharged emotion and ideas flood into the present even when you have no conscious recall of the original event. Once fully revisited and viewed they become normal memories that no longer cloud your vision. They have changed, vanished as etched impressions and become inert, the charged energy has dissipated and at this point they no longer have the power to harm you.

Attempting to go forward in the teeth of one of these old impressions is painful and arduous. Let us say your business has developed to the point where you need to do some public speaking, but you have an unreasonable and unreasoning terror of appearing foolish. Nothing anyone can do, or say, can convince you that you will not stand up and become a laughing stock. No amount of reassuring, cajoling, coercion or persuasion changes a thing. This stems from a time at school when you were verbally crucified in a debate and the whole class cackled like hens and teased you for months afterwards. Consciously you have managed to forget what was said and done, but the impression remains in place subconsciously along with your shock, mortification, shame and the resolution to never put yourself in a position where that could happen again. Until this psychic impression is located, revisited and re-evaluated and the charged energy dissipated, no force on Earth can convince you that you can speak in public comfortably. *Logically* there is no reason for you to fear a recurrence of the nightmare, you are no longer ten years old, you know your subject matter very well, your voice and appearance are presentable, and this is not a debate. None of these arguments matter when you have a psychic impression acting as a roadblock to your forward progress. The impression superimposes its painful energy on the present surroundings and dictates your reactions. So *emotionally* you are a quivering mass of nervous jelly.

It should be noted that abundance is not always a desirable thing, you want an abundance of the things you find desirable and a scarcity of those things you find undesirable. No one wants an abundance of cockroaches or tax audits.

When you are in or seeking to get into a position of power, you should state clearly and bear in mind exactly what you intend to create, be as specific as possible. Your thoughts have power; this can be a tough lesson to learn. If you do not clearly define what you want you may get your confused desire to manifest. If you are going to use your will to create a dream then you need to describe and visualize the dream as concisely as you can. What are you working to accomplish? What time frame can you realistically project for it? What resources will it take?

All projects contain energy, matter, space and time. Proper financing is one of the energies that make a business project viable. Oddly enough one can have too much financing and that is just as destructive as too little.

How can this be? How can one have too much financing?

Well, if you have too much borrowed money available in your start up, the tendency is to spend it all. This causes the business to be burdened with debt beyond its capacity to pay off quickly. This lengthens the time it takes for the business to become independently viable which in turn lengthens the time it takes to give you a return on your investment in it. Most of us will find ways to spend excess money. If we do not we can be sure our employees will! Robert Kiyosaki (Author of Rich Dad, Poor Dad) says there are two types of money problems: too much and too little. I think he is spot on!

Too little money causes stresses that I think are pretty obvious. Trying to make do with equipment that is inadequate comes immediately to mind. Or doing without the advertising and staff that are really essential for the tasks that have to be performed. I am sure you can think of others.

Exercises for Chapter Ten

1. Explain why positive thinking *alone* cannot work:

_____

_____

_____

_____

_____

_____

_____

2. Give examples of areas in your life that you dislike but that stay the same:

_____

_____

_____

_____

_____

_____

_____

_____

3. Take a look at possible reasons:

_____

_____

_____

_____

_____

_____

_____

_____

4. Give 3 examples of problems that could stem from too little financing:

_____

_____

_____

_____

_____

_____

_____

_____

_____
_____
_____

5. Give 3 examples of problems that could stem from too much financing:

_____
_____
_____
_____
_____
_____
_____
_____
_____
_____
_____
_____
_____

Chapter Eleven
THE MULTI-LEVEL MARKETING PHENOMENON

It is notable that in the last two decades various companies have sprung up using the multi-level pattern. This can to be an easy way for individuals to make the transition from employee to entrepreneur while eliminating many of the risks involved in starting up your own business. While few really succeed at it; those who merely do a little business on the side support those who really do make a success of it.

This type of business works on residual income where, as your down-line of distributors grows, income flows in from their sales augmenting whatever sales you make personally. There is often also a bonus system and commissions for starting new distributors.

The downside of this system is that usually the cost of the product has to be enough to spread the profit through many levels making it impossible to make much money on your personal sales, this naturally tends to make most products distributed in this manner either overpriced for its market, or when it is competitively priced there is little profit in it. This also forces the individual to recruit distributors, since you can't make a viable income off the sales alone.

The upside of it is that when there are few competitors and the product is good, it is easy to sell and to recruit distributors. Some, less than ethical, companies solve the difficulty by requiring their distributors to buy more products than they can honestly expect to move. This gives the company a false sense of security. False, because no company will be in business long without a product that is really selling to their public. A retail establishment that overstocks is in the same leaky boat.

One of the nice things about this type of business is that it can create *passive* income for you. Passive income is income that you do not directly produce by the sweat of your brow. It comes in whether you work or not.

Most people get into this type of business seeing it as a method of going into business for themselves without having to leave their day jobs. This, theoretically, allows them to take only the minor risk of their original investment whilst maintaining their security. The goal is usually to be self-employed rather than to be a business owner.

Well, risk is always part of a business venture, becoming successful at a business of this type takes a different type of risk. You have to learn to sell. This is where most people fall down, after running through their immediate family, fellow employees and friends, what is next? Oh God! Learning to talk to strangers! Learning to demonstrate the product and learning to sell and close sales.

If you have chosen a company with a good product which you really like and believe in, it is relatively easy to sell the product.

Selling the distributorships is an intangible and far more difficult for most people to accomplish. Many work away at it diligently, hoping against hope that one of their downline will be a marketing genius that will make them rich.

There is a hidden factor in becoming a successful marketer. People who are successful in business have a different mind-set to those who make good employees. One has to approach each endeavor with a different attitude. Entrepreneurs are always looking for investments with controlled risk. Employees are seeking security. The regular paycheck, the benefits, the pension plan, the medical coverage and paid vacations are foremost in their minds. Entrepreneurs have NONE of the above until they create them for themselves.

When one has a nice, safe, day job one is not hungry so there is no driving external factor to push one to ensure survival. One has to be motivated by desire, not by need, or fear of not making enough money to pay one's bills. Since most people whose bills for the month are covered would rather watch television than get out and do what it takes to widen their circle of acquaintances, inertia sets in. Usually, the networking companies try and bolster the flagging enthusiasm with rallies and meetings featuring motivational speakers and glowing testimonials. This is somewhat effective but does not help the person make the shift from pawn to player. It does not shift their attitude.

What DOES it take to be a success as a network marketer?

Well first of all it takes examining it as a business, not a hobby.

It is a good idea to crunch the numbers and see how much you have to create in order to make a consistent amount of money, enough to cover your basics and your upcoming need to invest in product stocks. How much product do you have to sell in order to make a reasonable income? How much does your average distributor actually sell each month. How many distributors will it take to sell that much product?

Once you have some approximate figures you can begin to set targets to reach your primary goal. The primary goal of any business is to be viable. Viable means: Able to stay afloat without assistance. Able to live. The second goal is to produce enough to pay YOU. The third is to pay you well for your investment of time and money.

When one does some assessing of the figures, it can look a bit overwhelming. One tends to keep plugging on hoping for some screaming genius to be recruited in your down line who will do it all for you. This is as effective as hoping to win the lottery, but never buying a ticket.

Marketing of any type is a numbers game. The more people you reach, the better are your chances of attracting some energetic players. However, having a lot of people doing a steady, if small, volume is the basic building block. If each individual distributor tries for this then your network has some stability.

Because marketing is a game of numbers, this means that YOU have to be able to make friends and inspire others, but most of all you need to have a strong desire to spread the word about this product line. The product or line of products itself has to be valuable in your opinion. It must be either unavailable elsewhere, or of a quality far surpassing what is widely available. You must have a reasonable certainty that the company you chose has good supply lines, that the products will continue to be available and there is excellent quality control on the products. Furthermore, you want to know that the company is financially strong and that your commission checks will be paid, and paid on time. Naturally, you would not wish to enroll, or enroll others, in a company with an unsteady financial foundation. This would violate your integrity and could, if the worst happened, damage your reputation.

Let us suppose that you have done your "due diligence" and looked into the products and the company itself and have found all is as it should be. Now you have decided to invest some time and money into forming your network.

There are those people who are open to your approaches and there are those who are not. In order to get started, most people quickly run through their family and close friends and that is where it stops. The considerations creep in as soon as one leaves the safe circle. "What will they think of me?" Will they think I am just out to take advantage of them?" "Will I lose their friendship?" "Will I lose their respect." "What if they say no?" I am sure you can think of more.

Well, what if they say no? Are you going to take it as a personal affront? Or could you *honestly* say "I want to show you this product and see what you decide?" When you can honestly say this, then you can stop worrying about what "they" will think of you because you know you are NOT pushing, coercing, cajoling or persuading. If your products are good, let them speak for themselves. There is no need to make yourself odious, in fact it is counter productive. The stereotypical salesman with his foot in the door is an old and very unpopular image. It certainly gave sales a bad name. So much so that today many people avoid any form of sales and some companies invent creative ways to get in the door. An example of this is a very expensive line of cookware whose pitch is to come and fix your dinner, hoping you will be so impressed you will pay thousands of dollars for pots and pans and fail to notice the slick way of getting past your guard.

Illustrating my point further, I wanted a water softener, so I called and made an appointment for the chap to come and sell me one. After a half hour of listening to him tell me how much money I would save if I invested in this product, I finally managed to get a word in edgewise. Irritated, I said rather sharply, "I asked you here so I could buy one, not to listen to your pitch, which is not particularly convincing anyway."

He was astounded.

His reasons for me to buy this product were all slanted to how much money I would save by spending $3500.00, when in fact, I wanted the softened water for health reasons and to protect the pipes in my old farmhouse home. He annoyed me so much he almost lost the sale. His arguments about how much money I would save in using less soap and shampoo were neither credible nor interesting to me. Perhaps he made sales because his clients would do ANYTHING to stop him from boring them to death.

Most salespeople TALK too much. Many people talk *at* you, too loudly and too long because they are nervous. If they allowed you to speak you might say no. Actually it is far better to find out what the prospective buyer thinks. If he has already made up his mind not to purchase, you can move on to someone else who has not. Additionally, if you allow your prospect to talk to you, you may find out what he is interested in, what he wants to solve and if your product could accommodate his needs.

I am sure all of us have been assailed with the prepared, memorized speech so popular with large corporations lately.

Did you find being gabbled at by a talking parrot encouraged you to buy anything?

I didn't think so.

This gives us a rule: don't chant at your prospects in a singsong manner. It offends them.

In this type of marketing, your customers fall into two categories, buyers of products and potential distributors. Products are tangible, distributorships are intangible. Do not assume that everyone fits in both categories. In general, it is necessary to listen to the person in order to establish which type you are talking to. There is of course some crossover. Trying to sell a distributorship to someone who merely wants the products and vice versa is both wasteful and time consuming.

Good products pretty much sell themselves, intangibles do not, and they take more explaining. Basically intangibles are ideas, visions, potentials and concepts. Intangible products are usually systems. This is where you can shine if you know your stuff. You must be fully familiar with the program, because what you are you are selling is the system. A system is a method of accomplishing something, a method that is reproducible. Others have used it successfully, you can too. Some multi-level marketing programs have better systems than others, but they all include product and distribution. Some give the salesperson a better cut and others favor the distributor. Some go down six levels, others more. Some require you to spend a certain amount each month to remain an active distributor, some do not. Some require a bigger initial investment than others. Most have a money back guarantee for dissatisfied customers. Some will ship from the warehouse directly to your customer and keep a database to ensure you are credited. Some even do your paperwork for you. The one thing none of them can do for you is *make* you successful. That is your job.

With all its pitfalls, network marketing is probably the least risky method of making the transition from employee to self-employed.

Few make it really big, but few lose their shirts either.

If you wish to be one of the few who make it big, then you must pay your dues in hard work, beating the bushes and in expenditure of time, just like any other new business. One of the big differences is that distributors are not employees, they are independent agents and they decide how much time and energy they will invest. This can be quite frustrating as it is up to you to raise the dead, so to speak, and get your down-line distributors into motion. There will be a percentage of people who really don't care to do much, they just want to get discounts for themselves and their family. There are others who do care, but can't seem to get off the ground. Most will be found to start off well then flounder on the rocks and shoals of criticism, rejection and disapproval. Some individuals are so scared of the rocks and shoals they project them into events before they happen, or do nothing, like a rabbit in the headlights they have paralyzed themselves with fear. This is a major obstacle for some people to overcome.

One should note that network marketing is not like owning a turnkey business; it won't run along without attention, LOTS of attention usually.

It remains the easiest and most fun method of easing from one mindset to another. If you are a people person, a good communicator, you will LOVE it.

Exercises for Chapter Eleven

1. Explain the difference between being self employed and owning a business:

   _____
   _____
   _____
   _____
   _____
   _____
   _____
   _____
   _____
   _____

2. Give three examples of tangible products:

   _____
   _____
   _____
   _____
   _____
   _____
   _____
   _____
   _____
   _____
   _____

3. Give 3 examples of intangible products:

   _____
   _____
   _____
   _____
   _____
   _____
   _____
   _____
   _____
   _____
   _____

_____
_____

4. Fill in the blank: "Most sales people _____too much."

5. If you are interested in this type of business:

* Examine how you feel about selling products

_____
_____
_____
_____
_____
_____
_____
_____
_____
_____
_____
_____

* Examine how you feel about recruiting distributors

_____
_____
_____
_____
_____
_____
_____
_____
_____
_____
_____
_____
_____
_____
_____

6. Then examine your lifestyle:
* Do you have lots of acquaintances? _____
* Do you make friends easily? _____
* Are you naturally interested in others? _____
* Are you a joiner? _____
* Can you have money? _____

If all your answers to 6 are yes then you should do well in this type of activity.

Chapter Twelve
DO YOU WORK FOR IT, OR DOES IT WORK FOR YOU?

When you are in business, or starting a business, it is a good idea to consider what you want from it.

What do you want it to do for you?

If you want it to provide you a place to do the things you want to do, as in the case of an artist who opens his own studio, or a hairdresser who wants his own salon, then you work for the business. It affords you the time and space to do what you want to do, but you are basically self-employed.

If you want to be in business in order to have the money or freedom to do something else, then you had better set it up so that it works for you, and then you are a business owner.

Many people embark into self-employment with the idea that they will have a great deal more freedom. This can be true, but only if you set it up that way.

Owning a business and running a business are birds of different feathers.

Each individual has his own Golden Nugget, the thing he most wants to do. It gives him or her satisfaction and a sense of harmony with the world.

Oddly enough, having lots of money is rarely the Golden Nugget. Lots of money is wonderful when it provides you with the wherewithal to do the things you really want to do. It has been noted by psychiatrists as well as in the media that there is a high incidence of mental problems, divorce, drug and alcohol abuse and suicides among the rich and famous. They have lots of money yet no purpose for it. No Golden Nuggets to make their lives worthwhile.

Few of us are born with the driving itch to be a painter like Picasso or a composer like Beethoven. We look at people like that and marvel at their lives. How wonderful it must be to live your dreams, we say wistfully. The big difference between them and others is not their wonderful talent, but that they knew what their dreams were!

Enid Vien

A person who has found his Golden Nugget is virtually unstoppable. Just TRY and stop him. He WILL not stop. He is living his dreams.

Each of us has some special thing that we yearn to do. It could be cooking delicious and nourishing meals, teaching the young, making systems run well or rocket science. Whatever it is, it is right for you. It does not have to be setting the world on fire with our blistering prose, or enchanting everyone with beautiful music. But when you find a way to make your Golden Nugget make you money so you can do it full speed ahead, that is blissful.

When we are young we often have great dreams of conquering the world in our own way. Dreams of wild success and fame and fortune fill our daydreams. School and "common sense" often knock that right out of us, and we end up living a life of drudgery and boredom. We sold out. Most of us, however, did not *completely* sell out. We are smart rats! We often find a way to make our dreams into hobbies, or find a job that enables us to utilize some part of our talents.

I have read many books that tell you that you can do anything you decide to do. What they don't say is that you will only decide to do those things that fit in with your basic nature. Not every person has the drive or desire to be a millionaire or entrepreneur. Not everyone wants to be a fireman or a nurse. I say, our diversity is wonderful!

I am SO happy someone else wants to be an engineer or scientist, I am glad to be me.

It is when we make the fatal compromises that we suffer the most. We stifle our dreams and talents doing things that do not give us a fair return. What can possibly pay you enough to give up your childhood dreams?

Mostly it is the search for security, the pursuit of money, which seduces us from our true purposes. It traps us in jobs we despise, gets us into doing things we consider less than ethical, or that we think are of little worth in our scheme of important things to do. Money alone will not make us happy, neither will a fancy car nor fine clothes. There has to be more to it. There is a joy that comes with earning our way through our own efforts, whether those efforts are physical or intellectual. When the money comes from earnings made through using our skills and talents, then the joy is increased tenfold.

Attitude plays a big part here, one can work for money, or one can make money work for you. I am not beating the drum here for investing ideas, although that may be a viable option for some. I am referring to making money provide you with the playing field in which to realize your dreams.

There is being what you want to be, doing what you want to do and having what you want to have. If you want to be a portrait painter, you will do what it takes to maintain that identity. What does a portrait painter do? He learns the skills, practices them and produces the portraits. He has the things necessary to paint the portraits. Then he has the

96

finished product that can be exchanged within the society for money. If painting portraits is his heart's desire, his Golden Nugget, then he will be happy and fulfilled.

If you own a business, then you can use it to afford you the time and energy to follow your dreams.

Often, our experiences have led us to believe we cannot do the things we would dearly love to be doing. Ridicule in school when we wrote our first halting essays or poems, painted our first pictures or flubbed our lines in the school play, is often the start of a nasty life trend. The things we love to do are so dear to us that we fear criticism of them. We take it very personally. These creative products contain a large part of our hearts and souls, so when they are treated with disdain or mockery we tend to retreat behind a screen or shell and do those socially acceptable things that will avoid such painful encounters. These are very bad lessons. They cut our reach for the stars and make us squash ourselves down into a mold in which we are very uncomfortable. We end up doing the conservative, no risk things; things which do not sing to our souls or gladden our hearts.

Some people have vocations to be in the healing field, or to teach. In the past, such positions rarely have paid much money. If it is what you really want to do, however, ways can always be found to make it work for you. I knew of a teacher who loved to teach. He had a business on the side buying real estate fixers. He loved to teach so much that he limited his real estate to the summer vacation time and in the summertime he made at least twice as much money as he did all year in his real job. This money enabled him to travel and have the things he wanted without sacrificing his Golden Nugget.

Leisure is a very over rated idea, yet leisure time can be made to work for you, just as money can. Leisure alone, with no purpose, can be quite deadly. We seem to have a deep, basic need to produce something of value to us. Often when people spend years saying all the things they will do when they retire, they do not do them. Instead, they rapidly deteriorate and die. They did not use the time to pursue their Golden Nuggets, or had long since given up on it.

Money can provide time and space, but if that time and space is not filled with productive energy, it will become a burden. If you have ever had time on your hands this will be very real to you. You often see this illustrated in the wives of wealthy men, whiling away their time in beauty parlors or endless rounds of shopping, none of which satisfies the empty void in their lives.

Being unproductive is spiritually quite deadening. So is spending your time producing things that you feel are of no value to anyone. One's self esteem suffers tremendously. Conversely, producing things of value to you and others raises the self-esteem enormously.

Exercises for Chapter Twelve

1. Write down the difference between you working for your business and your business working for you:

    _____
    _____
    _____
    _____
    _____
    _____
    _____
    _____
    _____
    _____
    _____
    _____

2. Give examples of people you know who are living their dreams:

    _____
    _____
    _____
    _____
    _____
    _____
    _____
    _____

3. Write a short essay on the relationship of productivity to self esteem:

    _____
    _____
    _____
    _____
    _____
    _____
    _____
    _____
    _____
    _____
    _____
    _____
    _____

Chapter Thirteen
COMPETITION

Competition! For many business owners the very word makes them shudder; they flinch from the idea that someone else's products are more attractive than their own and they fear the possible rejection that competition could mean. However, competition can be the breath of life in the marketplace, giving shoppers or potential clients power of choice and popularizing the product or idea in general.

Competition keeps us on our toes and demands of us that we make constant improvement, because failing to keep our eye on the ball can rapidly exclude us from the game entirely. If our prices, products or services are not competitive, then we will surely decline.

Usually we try and find a niche where we hope to have a monopoly. We are the sole distributor of some magical product, or the only manufacturer of special software, or the only one who creates this type of artwork, or furniture. Whatever it is we think it gives us that special edge. In this age of knowledge, we're not likely to hang onto that edge for long. Some smart rat will not only replicate our basic idea, he will improve on it, make it more cheaply, give it some special marketing angle and it's back to the drawing board for us. That is *if* we are clever enough to see it in time, clever enough to avoid hanging in there too long with a product that has become obsolete so rapidly that our heads are still spinning.

It is a law of this universe that nothing stays the same. Everything is either growing or contracting. We live in the world of constant motion, some visible some invisible. When we try to hold something still, hold onto a static pattern, we are trying to defeat the entire pattern of this universe and are eventually doomed to failure.

Businesses, like people, have a lifecycle. A good business with fine management can span quite a long time, especially if it rolls forward in time wisely, adjusting to the changes in the marketplace and always being in the forefront of any major advance in its field.

Competition, especially when it is good, is often necessary spur for us to improve, without it we are often inclined to stagnate and decay. We get in a comfortable rut and plod along with our heads down. When we are keenly aware of the competitive possibilities out in the world we do not allow ourselves the luxury of resting on our laurels in a comfortable rut. We push for excellence and we try to be out in front.

A system, such as the one we have in the USA, which is built on private enterprise, relies on competition for advancement in all fields. When you look at the accomplishments of the last century it is clear that there has been vast amounts of competition in many fields. The fastest growing area will be most often be found to be the one with the most competition; the slowest moving area is probably supported by government or even private subsidies.

In truth there is nothing wrong with a monopoly, it is *greedy* monopolies that are so harmful. A benevolent monarch is one type of monopoly. For as long as the benevolent leader holds power all goes well and people prosper, then his chinless son inherits and bleeds the country white with taxation. Or even in a Democracy, the new government comes in and wipes the slate of all the helpful reforms the previous government introduced. Governments are forms of monopoly and they detest that anyone else should hold similar powers so they attack other forms of monopoly. In civilized countries this is done by legislation, in others by pointing guns. Copyrights and patents are really legalized forms of monopoly. They protect authors and inventors (at least theoretically) for their lifetimes or longer in some cases.

There is no need to push yourself when you have no competitors. This explains why the USA has such rigorous laws regarding monopolies, and also why there are so many attempts to circumvent those laws. Monopolies inevitably lead to stagnation primarily due to the lack of motivation to create changes or improvements.

A greedy monopoly sets its own prices, makes its own rules and essentially holds society for ransom. I think we'll agree this is a Bad Thing. That is except when WE hold the monopoly, right?

Finding a niche in the marketplace is really finding a mini monopoly, or attaching one's business as a supplier of goods and services to a larger monopoly. Exclusive contracts are another form of mini monopoly. One seeks that spot where one can corner a piece of the market.

The real problem with monopolies is that they eventually become unstable. Either the people rise up and tear them down or a new idea renders them unnecessary. With mini monopolies often the contract is not renewed or some competitor offers a new variant that tempts the customer just as the monopoly holder became comfortable and complacent. Niches are only stable so long as the customer on whom one depends stays stable.

Realizing this does not make niches bad things to have. It just makes one aware that placing all one's eggs in one basket is as perilous in today's market place as it was way back when one carried eggs to market.

Exercises for Chapter Thirteen

1. Define the word monopoly:

   _____
   _____
   _____
   _____
   _____
   _____
   _____
   _____
   _____

2. Give examples of mini monopolies that work:

   _____
   _____
   _____
   _____
   _____
   _____
   _____
   _____
   _____

3. If you already have a business examine if you have a niche and if not look for what niche you could fill:

   _____
   _____
   _____
   _____
   _____
   _____
   _____
   _____
   _____
   _____
   _____
   _____

4. Explain the value of competition:

   _____
   _____
   _____
   _____
   _____

Enid Vien

Chapter Fourteen
FOOL'S GOLD

Gold is soft and malleable but strong, it endures very well, and it generally retains its value from one society to the next. Throughout our history gold has been valued for its beauty and its durability. Iron pyrite, also known as fool's gold, is very shiny, brittle and flaky. It is also much more common than gold. Gold is valuable and can be exchanged for currency; fool' s gold is worthless and cannot be exchanged for anything.

Unfortunately there's lots of fool's gold out there in the world of finance and business. Most of us stay away from the more obvious traps, but some are subtler than others, harder to see, many are seductive and secure in appearance. Many of us have fallen in these traps and have not yet noticed that we are in them. An example of this is low interest-bearing deposit accounts, commonly known as CDs. They pay you interest, yes, but the interest rate is so low that the return on your investment is actually lower than the inflation rate. This means you are really *losing* money because your money is declining in value while the bank is investing it in high yield propositions and making the money YOU could have been making if you had looked around a bit more.

Meanwhile, because you have locked your money in a vault, you use high interest-bearing credit cards for major purchases. This means you are paying out interest substantially higher than that generated by your CDs. Not the most favorable situation because this keeps you trapped in a treadmill of debt, all the while believing you have a nice secure investment. This is one example of fool's gold. It looks so nice and shiny, but it evaporates your hard earned cash like so much dust in the wind. When you eventually go to use the money from your CD you find its purchasing power has sharply declined. Amazingly, we're not is horrified by this is we should be because we have been living in the society and prices have risen slowly enough that we didn't notice it. We rarely sit down and figure out what we could've bought with the money five years ago when we deposited it, so we think that it grew in amount, but alas, 'tis merely fool's gold.

Well, you say, what else can I do?

Examining the arithmetic of any transaction is certainly a good start. Anything you buy that has payments containing compound interest needs especially fine scrutiny. For example not all CDs are below the rate of inflation, just most of them.

Though the year as I have seen so many people with get-rich-quick schemes, many of which are on the fringes of illegality and *appear* very clever but collapse under their own weight very rapidly. Most such schemes when examined are based on faulty arithmetic, they add in factors that are not present and omit factors that are present. The person with the scheme wants it to work so badly that he subconsciously rigs the deck and so fools himself and others with his erroneous figures. The intention and conviction of the person with the plan is really not the issue, it is the arithmetic that tells the tale. With the best intention in the world any proposed business or investment cannot succeed if it is not making more than it spends and that includes paying back its investors.

Most often businesses have hidden costs that are difficult to determine. At one time David and I had a trucking company that was generating huge amounts of money every week, unfortunately, it was also generating huge costs. The problem was how to make a reasonable profit. We never did really solve this problem; we just worked harder, and harder, and harder until we practically collapsed.

The golden rule of finance is:

Generate more money than you spend.

How *much* more depends on what extra expenses or emergencies are likely in your particular business or family. On examination you will find many businesses fall in the barely solvent category, their outgo and income are far too close together for comfort. This is a danger signal. When the operating expenses are too high, any large and unexpected expense throws them into debt and all of a sudden their cash cow becomes a pet elephant. (Pet elephants being enormously expensive to feed.)

It is amazing how few business people know their operating expenses clearly. What does it take to operate your business for a day? The hidden expenses and those that only come around quarterly need to be included in a cost analysis in order to see clearly what one day's expenses really are.

When emergency expenditures show up it is very tempting to borrow money.

Borrowed money is almost always fool's gold. Loans, whether from a bank or from investors, almost always carry a heavy price. The initial price of the loan is frequently added onto the loan itself and hidden within the payments so that you scarcely notice that the borrowed money is costing you well in excess of its actual value. Very short-term loans that are paid off before the first payment still costs you, but not nearly as much, and these can be very useful in consummating certain deals. This works, but when you intend to slog along making interest payments, take a second look before you commit yourself and your business. A good question to ask yourself is: Will the borrowed money help you generate more production or sales? Loans lock you into a future laden with payments and debt. You feel (temporarily) wealthy and so tend to overspend on trivia that does not bring in income.

This tends to ensure the wealth is temporary.

It is fool's gold again. Fool's gold is wealth you only *think* you have.

Exercises for Chapter Fourteen

1. If you have a business, do a cost analysis including all expenses:

    _____
    _____
    _____
    _____
    _____
    _____
    _____
    _____
    _____
    _____

2. How solvent is your business?

    _____
    _____
    _____
    _____
    _____
    _____
    _____
    _____

3. If a piece of equipment broke tomorrow could you afford to repair or replace it without borrowing?

    _____
    _____
    _____
    _____
    _____
    _____
    _____
    _____

4. What is the Golden Rule of finances?

    _____
    _____
    _____
    _____
    _____
    _____

_____
_____
_____
_____

5.   If you are thinking of borrowing money what question should you ask yourself?

_____
_____
_____
_____
_____
_____
_____
_____
_____

Chapter Fifteen
CHARISMATIC CHARMERS

After a chapter dedicated to fool's gold it seems to follow naturally that I should write a chapter on charismatic charmers. Such people are masters of illusion. These people actually fall in the pretense band but are worthy of a closer look. These are extreme, almost archetypal examples of pretenders.

It is very difficult to spot charismatic charmers because they believe their own illusions. They tell themselves a story and get lost in their own wonderful creation. They invent a character for themselves that is magical, invincible and marvelous. For a person to be able to do this he would have to have vast amounts of Dynamis at his disposal. It is a tragic peculiarity that with so much Dynamis at his disposal he actually could be what he is pretending to be, but his psychic wounds make this impossible. Under the glossy façade is a very alienated individual. This becomes obvious when the house of cards falls down. There is not a lot of integrity here, so under duress the person commits acts that no person of conscience would ever do.

Persons in the pretense band are motivated by fear. They hang between the fear band and the aggression band. They are too afraid to be aggressive and express their hatred, envy and contempt openly. They are a long, long, way from being in contact with who they truly are. So they produce a smokescreen, pretend to be larger than life, more perfect than perfect, the ideal man or woman. It really *is* too good to be true.

Such individuals are often found in religions or cults, they seem to delight in enlightenment fields where they can promote themselves as The Enlightened One. I suppose this is a form of megalomania. They are also, unfortunately, frequently found in investment opportunity businesses, where they may be found promoting and selling fool's gold.

It is really quite a shame that such people are so difficult to classify and identify, because they give their victims deep and enduring psychic wounds. After someone has received a psychic wound in which a charismatic charmer betrayed them, damaging their trust, they frequently go to the other extreme and become extremely distrustful of every opportunity that comes their way.

Enid Vien

I have written quite a bit on the subject of Secretive Wounded Birds in my book Mood Swings. The Secretive Wounded Bird has so many soul scars that he or she has developed a false personality that SEEMS very nice. While the charismatic charmer does fit in this category, he or she stands out because of the enormous quantities of life energy this person has. This person is so powerful that he is actually riding on the high swing of the mood-swings pendulum. This high swing may last a very long time due to the amount of power that is maintaining it. Inevitably, eventually it does crash and the person goes into the opposite mode, the reverse swing of the pendulum. Once the person has sunk into the lower mood he may stay there for a long time. This same amount of energy that was maintaining the high mood is now maintaining the low mood. So the individual may go into a very deep depression, or a very deep state of shame, even become suicidal.

From our point of view the important thing is how do we detect such individuals and distinguish them from a truly creative and causative person that could make a huge difference in our lives.

I have given this great deal of thought. Like anyone else, I have a regrettable tendency to display the "Once bitten, twice shy" Syndrome. Of course this makes a great deal of sense, but it is tremendously limiting. It has a tendency to trap one in the bland band being very conservative and very self-protective.

So how *do* you detect and categorize the charismatic charmer?

1. On first meeting him, he may seem too good to be true.

2. Generally, such people seem to be moving very quickly, almost in a manic state.

3. He has grandiose ideas.

4. He talks a lot about his own successes and cleverness, if he is in the Enlightenment field he will probably talk a great deal about his wondrous and significant ascension experiences.

5. He holds the attention; in fact he hogs it.

6. He appears to be everything anyone would ever want to be. He is the epitome of all the virtues of the ideal person within the sphere in which he is operating.

7. He sparkles and spreads fairy dust on the eyes of his beholders.

8. He is very good at telling people what to think. (In order to maintain an illusion it is necessary to ensure that others are thinking along the same lines, this way those around the charismatic charmer actually help him to maintain the illusion.)

9. He is very persuasive but appears to do it without effort.

10. He is addicted to adoration, admiration and praise.

11. He is narcissistic.

12. If you watch carefully there are moments when another personality briefly emerges which does not have the confidence and happiness that he normally displays.

13. He commits petty acts that are not too ethical, and you find yourself making excuses for him. Well you say, anybody can have a bad day.

14. He believes he is invincible, Godlike, or in touch with the Godhead.

15. Sometimes he thinks his very presence will cause everything to miraculously be transformed.

16. You are sometimes uncertain if he is kidding or not.

The fact is that we ignore the clues, because we want him so badly to be real. We want to believe that he can lead us to Enlightenment, or to wealth or understanding. It is our own desire to be what he is, do what he does, have what he has, that blinds us to the reality. We are actually contributing to the house of cards.

When we contribute money, energy and that intangible thing called belief to one of these charismatic charmers and later the house of cards falls down we feel very betrayed. It is hard to see our own responsibility in this situation and its outcome. We feel like innocent victims, and we feel we were made foolish. It is very hard to examine one's own inadequacies and motives that allowed us to be deceived.

So, usually we adopt new policies to prevent anything like that from happening again. These new policies are generally of the type that sticks us firmly in conservatism, squarely in the bland band. Resolutions to be more careful, to check the fine print, to only trust family members, to invest in established institutions, are a few examples of this train of thought.

Difficult as it is to get out of these limiting thought patterns, they are really not the answer. In the final analysis only good judgment and the ability to tell the difference between a genuine genius and a charismatic, charming charlatan is the answer.

Exercises for Chapter Fifteen

1. Give some examples of Charismatic Charmers:

   _____
   _____
   _____
   _____
   _____
   _____
   _____
   _____
   _____
   _____

2. What are some of the symptoms that would allow you to spot one?

   _____
   _____
   _____
   _____
   _____
   _____
   _____
   _____
   _____
   _____
   _____
   _____

Chapter Sixteen
SELECTING MENTORS

In our search for excellence, mentors become a very necessary part of our lives. When one wishes to become a master at anything, whether it be investing, running a business, producing works of art, writing a book, one needs to be constantly involved in the process of learning. This means you have to admit to yourself that you do not know everything. This admission is the doorway to mastery.

A mentor is really a teacher, as well as an adviser and trainer. In any new endeavor one doesn't start out as a master. Ideally one starts out as an apprentice.

So, how do you select the right mentor for the right subject?

How do you know that you are not just choosing a charismatic charmer?

The key is in the prospective teacher's involvement with the subject.

A true master of any craft or field is constantly practicing, reading up on it, staying abreast of new developments, learning new techniques; in short, he is involved deeply in his chosen subject. A false master is merely teaching what he most needs to learn. He can only teach; he cannot do.

If you wish to become a master at anything it is necessary to truly connect with the subject. You cannot dig a ditch without picking up a shovel, or hit consistent homeruns without practicing.

Subjects that require a great deal of theory are harder for most people to grasp. We are generally not taught how to study for application; however we are usually very well grounded in the parrot techniques necessary to pass exams. The keys to learning for application are really quite simple although quite exacting.

The Keys:

1. Every subject has it's own vocabulary, and it is necessary to fully understand the specialized terms used within the subject.

2. This means one must be able to define each term, use it correctly in speech, and explain it to somebody else so that they can understand it.

3. This has involved your intellect. Now you must involve yourself further and learn the necessary workings of the terms you have learned. You can draw them out on paper; use diagrams or charts, even make working models in order to get a deeper understanding.

4. Now that you have grasped some of the specialized terminology you must now study the broad general principles that govern the subject.

5. These broad general principles can also be reduced to diagrams and models. The rule of thumb is that if you cannot demonstrate it, you cannot use it. You do not know it well enough.

In looking around to find the mentor that you need first really look at the person and judge him or her by the following criteria:

> Does he walk his walk or merely talk it?
> Is he intimately involved with the development of his subject?
> Does he think he knows it all, or is he still *actively* learning?

The key word is "actively." To learn is a verb. That means you have to DO something. All subjects evolve and grow. You want a mentor who is actively learning.

Recently, a person came to my attention that had caused many others quite a lot of grief. He had touted himself as a mentor and a great many people lost large sums of money by taking his advice because he appeared so successful, so clever, and was so charming. After the disaster I sat down with several of those involved and we analyzed his behavior with a nice large rearview mirror. It became quite clear that this person was not doing the things he claimed to be an expert at. In short, he was not a master of the subject at all. He may have been a master of misdirection, of smoke and mirrors, of seduction and deceit, but he certainly wasn't a master of the subject that he claimed to be.

One of my friends said: "In retrospect, I noticed that he would not discuss and never seemed to be doing anything in the area where he claimed to have such huge successes. He always seemed to be doing something else. I didn't think much about it at the time."

I think, I hope, I would have been more curious.

Certainly, he did not exemplify our criteria for a master or a mentor.

1. He was not working at it.
2. He was not intimately and deeply involved with his subject.

These two criteria had they been first known and second examined, would have excluded him from that position.

It is an oddity that I rather like that true masters have a passion for their subject. They do not just talk about the subject; they live it. Would you rather learn from somebody who is in love with his topic, or from someone who knows a lot about the subject secondhand?

A true master knows his topic.

Knowing the topic and *knowing about* the topic are distinctly different. This is a very important distinction.

I know about fine china; I do not know how it is made, or the criteria by which it is judged.

A master would know fine china inside and out. He would know enough to know when he doesn't know a specific datum and he would know where to find it. In short he knows when he knows and he knows and admits it when he doesn't.

Exercises for Chapter Sixteen

1.   How would you recognize a master at any subject?

_____

_____

_____

_____

_____

_____

_____

2.   How does one choose a mentor?

_____

_____

_____

_____

_____

_____

_____

3.   What is the doorway to mastery?

_____

_____

_____

_____

_____

_____

_____

Chapter Seventeen
BREAKING THE MOLD

We all form a view of ourselves when we are young. We learn the patterns we're taught by families and schools and unfortunately we *also* learn self-limiting factors as we go along.

We learn what we can and cannot have, what we can and cannot ask for, what one of our station in life may or may not do. Women, for example, can only hold certain positions, or command certain salaries; various ethnic groups are typecast into menial positions and so on. We learn by a sort of psychic osmosis what is acceptable and unacceptable from us, and we set invisible ceilings according to the lessons we are subliminally learning. It is a rare being that can examine and discard these early lessons without having them pointed out to them. Sometimes we react in reverse mode, our parents were wealthy so we must be poor, or our parents were poor so we must prove ourselves by becoming wealthy. More commonly though, we attempt only those things we see as realistic within our worldview, without realizing that our worldview was a picture painted for us by others, or painted by ourselves during our childhood. It seems it should not be necessary to say that ideas formed at age three are often very inappropriate at thirty-three, but it *is* necessary. These ideas run under one's surface thoughts like the operating system under windows in a computer.

It is a source of constant amazement to me, the things that people can keep on believing!

It is a further source of amazement when I find some lingering limiting belief in myself!

It is understandable when one realizes these are not clearly visible to the individual and so they escape inspection.

I was born in wartime; in my early years soap was at a premium, when you could get it at all. Recently, yes RECENTLY, I found myself carefully using up every last scrap of a soap that I should not be using on my sensitive skin, rather than opening the special new soap that was sitting unopened on the shelf. I was making myself suffer in order not to waste soap! Soap is VALUABLE, you see. I had to laugh at myself. The soap had an invisible label on it that said, "I am not to be wasted under any circumstances." It made me wonder exactly what else I had learned in wartime that was still dictating my behavior today! So I began to look at my habit patterns and sort out which ones had derived from those early experiences.

Certainly I learned one should, wherever possible, fix or do things oneself. Repairmen were scarce because most of the younger men were off fighting in the war and minor details did not count for much when bombs were falling nightly. Why fix the house when it might be bombed out of existence tomorrow? Today, this has translated into doing as much as possible myself, my own typesetting, illustrations, the cooking, painting the house, the general attitude being one of thrift and self-reliance. I also have an annoying tendency not to bother with maintenance until something breaks or otherwise forces itself upon me. The thrift and self-reliance sounds nice, yes, but actually it's very limiting. It does not take into account of my time as a valuable commodity, a mold that I am now learning to break. It makes a lot more sense to employ an expert to do things which they have perfected and for me to concentrate on those things at which I excel.

I also realized that my tendency to want to do only those things which I can control stemmed from the dreadful, out of control feeling that bombs dropping, seemingly at random, inspired in me. This was programming that was not visible to me for a very long time.

In such circumstances it seems natural to conclude that people cannot be trusted at all when outside your influence. You are learning that the only safety possible is to be influential, set a good example and hope to be out of the way when entire nations decide to have a temper tantrum and attack their neighbors. This was one *very* destructive lesson. A lesson that has led me into many good things yet has also kept me from a lot of fun and co-operation throughout this lifetime. Being under fire can certainly etch patterns on one's soul affecting one's entire life from then on out. That is until one brings them out into the light of day for inspection and reevaluation.

When I thoroughly examined this it became clear to me that the idea that people could be wantonly destructive had the following consequences:

1. It got me into studying philosophy, religion and psychiatry, psychology, sociology and the all the various branches of each in the effort to find a way to eradicate such violence and insanity.
2. It made me a bit of a loner.
3. It made me very suspicious of any form of mind control including rabble-rousing speeches, manipulation, guilt trips, and all the myriad subtle pressures to "believe" in this or that, or to think this way or that.
4. It made me highly nervous about all group agreements, especially those that say one race, religion, country club or country; is better or worse than another.
5. It made me a freethinker.

6. It made me practically impervious to advertising.
7. It drove me to study what made people tick, and what runs down their clocks.
8. It made me independent to a fault.
9. It honed my intellect making me rather deadly in debate.
10. It gave me a purpose in life that was so important to me I could let other aspects of life slide into neglect.
11. It pushed me into acquiring a huge vocabulary at a very young age so that I could understand the monster books I wanted to read.
12. It made me reluctant to join any group or organization that I was not controlling. I could never be just one of the gang or blindly give my devotion or loyalty.
13. I could not become a psychologist or psychiatrist or scientist for to do so required me to agree with the very fields that I saw as spawning the insanity not solving it.
14. I am thrifty in minor things, extravagant in others (not so minor).
15. I can make a marvelous meal when others swear there is nothing in the larder.
16. I am extremely resourceful and can fix almost anything.
17. I am highly intolerant of intolerance. (Isn't that an oxymoron?)
18. I detest arrogance.
19. I will take charge situations and I will have things my way, nicely, of course.
20. It made me inclined to sympathize and identify with the spunky underdog and be irritated by the whining victims of this world.

In short, my early childhood had shaped my entire life. This was quite a revelation to me. It is not, of course, that people cannot be wantonly destructive at times, they certainly can. It is having that idea subconsciously adding into every situation on a sub-aware level, along with the anxiety of not knowing when or where the next bombs would fall, that is so deadly.

On the surface, many of those things I listed seemed like good lessons, yet in practice they were a two edged sword in many ways.

I could not commit fully to anyone or to any group, for I knew there was potential insanity lurking in the depths of their mental cellars. I could not relax; a lifetime is far too short for the task I had set myself. I ran down many blind alleys, I was driven to understand, to discover; it was a burning, all-consuming passion. I could not live a simple life, work at a simple job or be swayed in any way from my chosen path. I was in a rigid box of my own contrivance. Once I realized all this, I was in a position to change those things that I thought should be changed, to keep in place the things I liked, and I could reconstruct my entire existence into what I wanted my life to be. Amazing, isn't it?

It was interesting to note that I have also found it very difficult to take instruction from anyone; I *had* to learn for myself. I really had very little choice in the matter. My distrust of others deep-seated mental capabilities and intentions, especially those of which they were unaware, made this essential. I knew in my heart that not everyone had the evil seeds of destruction lurking within them, but I had no way to know who did and who did not.

As a very young child, I had concluded that all the adults, especially the males, had the evil seeds within. They taught us, the children, not to smack each other when they were hurling artillery at each other. This made them appear deceptive, hypocritical, less than honest with themselves and certainly deluding themselves about us children. The children in kindergarten certainly would have cheerfully torn each other limb from limb without adult intervention. This seemed to prove that the seeds of destruction were present in all of us. Those that appeared not to have them were probably just too scared to act either to attack or defend. This seemed very logical. Meanwhile I set about trying to teach the teachers; don't hit, be polite, don't bully us, try and understand; I am still doing it today.

Naturally, when I eventually learned about the depths of depravity to which the Nazis had sunk with their death camps and their ethnic cleansing, this served to reinforce my existing conviction that humanity had a Fatal Flaw.

All of this went against my naturally basic love and trust of people. So I was torn. I had a personal war waging within me that has, at times, almost destroyed my life. Although, I must say, my love of people is so great that I never became embittered. I really never indulged in attempting to place blame. My saving grace was I always looked for the seeds within myself in order to eradicate them and so improve myself.

Somewhere along the line I learned that we make our lives from who we are. Had I not been a naturally loving person, I might have pursued ways to wreak destruction upon the destructive, to build a bigger and better bomb. Instead, I pursued the idea that evil and insanity is not us, not who we really are, and that we can cleanse ourselves of it and get back to our true nature. This is how I arrived at clearing and personal coaching as a profession. Loving others is part of my makeup, part of who I am. Acting in a distrusting manner is not natural to my personality; it twists my life energy into unnatural patterns that are very uncomfortable and personally destructive. If I had not recovered these childhood memories and faced them, I might never have broken out of that mold that I created when I was a frightened kid listening to the nightly drone of German bombers.

Exercises for Chapter Seventeen

1.   Examine your own patterns:

        _____
        _____
        _____
        _____
        _____
        _____
        _____
        _____
        _____
        _____
        _____
        _____

2.   What habits are ruling your behavior?

        _____
        _____
        _____
        _____
        _____
        _____
        _____
        _____

Chapter Eighteen
UNLOCKING YOUR POTENTIAL

We are locked into thought patterns that we formed during our compulsory attendance at life's "School Of Hard Knocks." In places where we already have one of these thought patterns installed it is almost impossible to learn anything new. The new idea cannot get in to the place where it would fit because that place is already occupied. Sometimes, the individual tries to merge the old and the new into an unhappy marriage. The old ideas are often locked in place by pain or painful emotion, giving one a mindset that seems to be carved in stone. In those areas where one has one of these grooves in one's thinking one cannot learn, grow or change. We try and change our habits but fail miserably because we cannot get out of the groove. We try to overlay our old ideas with new ones without fully examining and discarding the old ones first. So, when we get under stress we either revert back to the old ideas and those old patterns, or we become paralyzed with indecision because the two ideas cannot be reconciled.

If school was arduous and stressful there will be many areas that inhibit our success in business and indeed any area of life later on.

Joe was teased unmercifully at school. This ruined his concentration and his grades suffered. That earned him a beating from his dad who believed that you can and should try to knock sense into children's heads. In later years, whenever he had to study something he felt scared and humiliated before he even began to study it. He concluded he had an unsolvable study problem and so he limited himself to work that required little or no book learning. This put a considerable cramp in his style. He had to depend on others for many things, for example accounting. This in itself would not have been so bad, but he felt inadequate to even *oversee* the work. Naturally this left him at the mercy of unscrupulous accountants and employees. Eventually he gave up being in business and took a job where he did not have to deal with any of that.

Mary had a fear of offending that stemmed from an abusive childhood where any hint of self-willed action was severely punished by her ferociously overprotective parents. This resulted in a rather self-effacing personality. Mary would take no action that she thought might cause an upset. She opened a flower shop and had two employees upon whom she relied to make all the decisions for her. This worked for awhile, but they also made the decisions about how much they should be paid and were rather generous with the flowers to the point where the shop was rapidly becoming insolvent. Mary simply could not say no to them. Fortunately she married a chap who could and did say no and the situation was reversed. The trouble was she felt dreadful when the employees became upset and she nagged him about being so harsh with them. He felt that she did not appreciate his efforts to save her bacon. Their marriage suffered. Her driving need to be liked, and therefore safe from attack, had made her quite incompetent to lead or even to allow another to lead in a decisive manner. Ironically, with her obsessive desire to placate others she alienated the person she loved the most and who was most important to her happiness.

Tom was a do-it-yourself type, a perfectionist. He gave people jobs and could not leave them alone to do them. He had no faith in their ability or judgment and they could certainly sense it. He often wondered why he could not keep any staff. His obsessive need to oversee everything kept him in a small loop that none of his intentions to expand could crack. This habit had originated at home where he had learned it from his father. His father frequently said, "If you want something done right, you have to do it yourself." He had a secondary song he sang that went "You can't trust anyone else to do things the way you would do them." The problem with a mindset like that is that it becomes a self-fulfilling prophecy, with every error being duly noted is proof positive that the idea is correct.

Colin was an athlete at school and learned that you can always succeed if you just overwhelm the opposition with more effort and forcefulness. This worked very well in the boxing ring; it was much less successful when selling insurance. So he worked harder, and he worked harder, he worked longer hours and he pushed himself more and more. He became more and more forceful with his customers who tried to avoid him as much as possible. He refused to quit because he KNEW he could do anything if he just worked hard enough and put more effort in it. Eventually he gave himself a heart attack and was forced to quit.

In each of the examples described above, none of those people could change. Their fixed ideas presented them from learning and making a change. The key ideas defied inspection because they were "givens." A "given" is an idea that one does not inspect because it is so much a part of one's thinking that one never even considers it. One KNOWS it is right. In any area where one cannot seem to grow or improve, despite heroic efforts, it is reasonable to suspect that one has a crop of "givens" sprouting in the basement of one's mind.

Your success depends upon your ability to discover and inspect these "givens." I called it weeding out the basement. Most of us require help with this; rare individuals can do it naturally. For the rest of us, less fortunate people, a personal coach or clearing practitioner who can guide us through the jungle is essential.

Dynamis coaching and clearing is based on the idea that you really do know what you are doing and thinking, you have simply buried the knowledge. In times of stress, loss or anguish you came to conclusions and learned lessons that are no longer appropriate to the circumstances. You formed operating principles based on these conclusions and lessons. They probably did work for you at the time, but they are definitely working against you now. They have become blocks, barriers, or invisible ceilings. You just can't quite put your finger on them. Discovering, uncovering, and re-examining these old lessons is essential for learning new ones.

LESSONS

Some people go through life believing that every setback, and every event contains a lesson, and it does. It is just that some of these are *bad lessons* that teach us unworkable principles that hold us back from our full potential.

I have a friend who thinks that all adversity is sent by God and is intended to teach her some lesson and that life is orchestrated by Him with that in mind. I thoroughly disagree. I can't imagine a benevolent creator torturing his children as a Lesson! That is more demoniacal than otherwise. I have seen some men do this, yelling: "I'll teach you to_____!" as they grabbed their belts or a switch. What benefit could possibly come from such abuse? What exactly is the child supposed to learn?

Not all lessons are helpful and good.

Indoctrination, propaganda and prejudice are extreme examples of bad lessons. They are often learned only too well!

When Father was drunk and violent Fay learned to be a little mouse, to keep her mouth shut and slink up to her room. It saved her from further abuse at the time. Unfortunately, today she is still a little mouse with her husband and children. They do not understand it; it makes them feel very confused, even hurt at times, when she acts as though they are ogres who might bite. It can be quite unnerving to be around someone who vanishes or capitulates at the first sign of disagreement. Naturally the children capitalized on this when they were younger and now feel rather guilty about the way they treated her.

These are examples where, under threat or heavy duress, certain lessons were learned far too well and they became engraved within the individual's consciousness where they act as constant inhibitors. These lessons are the chains that bind us, teaching us to lie rather than confess when we err, teaching us to distrust or fear and worst of all teaching us how to become abusers ourselves. I bet there is not a human alive today who does not have an excellent role model for an abuser. Sadly, there are many who do not have an excellent role model for successful, harmonious living. All this prevents us from reaching out for a star to swing on; keeps us from living up to our potential, and locks us firmly in our boxes.

I reiterate, not all lessons are helpful and good! However, a bright, optimistic person can often turn lemons into lemonade.

Exercises for Chapter Eighteen

1. Examine some of the bad lessons you have learned:

   _____
   _____
   _____
   _____
   _____
   _____
   _____
   _____
   _____
   _____
   _____
   _____
   _____
   _____
   _____
   _____
   _____

2. Take them one at a time and ask yourself "What has been the consequences of this belief?"

   _____
   _____
   _____
   _____
   _____
   _____
   _____
   _____
   _____
   _____
   _____
   _____
   _____
   _____
   _____

Chapter Nineteen
INTEGRITY IN BUSINESS

Business runs on trust. Any contract, any agreement, any relationship, all have trust as their basis. When you put your money in a bank, use a credit card, buy a house; you are exercising trust. When trust breaks down, so does the business. In many businesses the business owner has to deliver the service or goods before he is paid, he has to trust the customer to keep his end of the bargain.

A more fundamental aspect of trust is our money. We trust that it is worth something. It is really only a piece of printed-paper that *represents* a unit of exchange. The value fluctuates daily in response to world market conditions. In our daily lives we are rarely aware of this. We tend to think our dollar or pound is worth as much on one day as the next. We judge it by our purchasing power and that is a workable enough yardstick most of the time. We do not realize when we buy something that in doing so we are trusting our governments to maintain the world exchange rate and adjust the values of these pieces of paper. Maintaining the values of money that is not based on a gold or other tangible standard is an elaborate juggling act requiring much careful analysis and manipulation.

We *trust* that written documents mean what they say and we trust (blindly in most cases) that our money is worth what it states on the front. We have to do this or all commerce breaks down. When people lose their trust in a bank or a government the institution falls very quickly. This intangible asset called trust is the most valuable possession any business can own.

All transactions involve trust. A business or any organization builds trust by being trustworthy. Essentially this means deliver what you say you will deliver when you say you will deliver it. For a service it means do what you say you will do when you say you will do it. If you cannot do so, inform the customer or client at the earliest opportunity. If you do not then you forfeit their trust. Some salespeople make rash promises in order to close a sale; this almost always backfires. Apart from being dishonest, this is a very bad business policy because it destroys trust.

In today's world with its rapid pace many people habitually break their word. A broken appointment, an extra-marital affair, broken contracts, failure to call back after saying one will, these breed an atmosphere of distrust. It seems to tell us that our business is not important when we do not get the call back or the follow up to our requests for information.

Little white lies are another great trust destroyer. We frequently run into the social agreement that says it is okay to deceive others in minor ways. It appears to smooth things over and to maintain a calm environment, at least on the surface. We sometimes get in the habit of social lying, it seems to keep the person mollified and prevent confrontations. It is deadly however when the person finds out he has been handed a lollipop.

No one likes being pacified.

Trust is destroyed at this point.

How do you build trust in business? You stay in communication. You let the customer or client know what is going on and show him or her your concern. You do your very best to keep your word and to do so in a timely manner. When you cannot keep an appointment or do what you intended on time you *tell* the person as soon as possible. This builds a relationship in which trust can grow.

Exercises for Chapter Nineteen

1. Write a short essay on how to build trust:

_____
_____
_____
_____
_____
_____
_____
_____
_____
_____
_____
_____
_____
_____
_____
_____
_____
_____
_____
_____

2. Explain what trust has to do with success:

_____
_____
_____
_____
_____
_____
_____
_____
_____
_____
_____

Chapter Twenty
CLEARING THE BLOCKS TO SUCCESS

What is Case? It is the bringing into the present of old emotional baggage, misunderstandings and [1]righteous computations and superimposing them upon the current surroundings.

When something in the present is perceived to have some similarity, or even potential similarity, to an unpleasant experience in the past, a gateway can open to that experience and all the emotions and ideas it contains will gush into the present.

The individual as spirit, that is to say the essential YOU, is pure, perfect and whole. Unpleasant experiences alter that purity and the accumulation of these experiences accompanied by the decisions, conclusions, resolutions, and emotions along with the creations that they bring about, comprise the case.

When you perceive something in the present has some similarity, or even a possible chance of becoming similar to an earlier unpleasant experience, a gateway opens to that experience. All the emotions and ideas that the old experience contains come gushing into the present where they influence your behavior while remaining unseen and unsus-

---

[1] 1. Righteous computations and self-fulfilling prophecies have much in common. They are both supposed to solve the possibility of future psychic wounds, to nip them in the bud before they happen. You could think of them as psychic alarm bells.
2. The righteous computation is a fixed idea that the individual believes gives him an advantage, keeps him out of trouble and enhances his chances of survival as well as keeping him in control. Often the major righteous computation of this lifetime is formed when the person is quite young and vulnerable. It is designed to protect him and answer why everything is the way it is. Since it is unlikely that any of us can really come up with the ultimate answer to existence when we are three or four years old, many of these ideas seem hilariously funny once they are unearthed and examined. The anguish the child felt at the time of its making locks the computation in place, imprinting it on his consciousness.

Enid Vien

pected. Sometimes one wonders if one is overreacting. So when a person is acting with more emotional reaction than the circumstances appear to call for, it is often a [2]psychic recording from the past adding into the present without his conscious knowledge. Usually the individual is vaguely aware that he or she is acting irrationally, and feels driven to continue treating those around him or her as though they were the persons who hurt him in the past or to act in the manner decided long ago when he was under tremendous stress.

When the incident so activated is really severe, it may become more real to the individual than his actual surroundings, in which case he or she becomes temporarily deranged. Anything you say or do at these times will become part of the scene that is replaying, except being very quiet and calm. Quite often after an episode like this the person cannot quite remember what happened, or later insists that you said and did things that you are absolutely positive you did not do. This can be very confusing until you realize that this is part of the old recording superimposing itself over the present circumstances.

When you see this happening you may try telling the person that something from the past has become reactivated. Sometimes this cools it off. If you sense that YOU are overreacting, it's a good idea to go for a walk, or a swim or simply stare at the ocean until you contact your present surroundings again. Do *something* to move out of the old drama. Every time you rant and rave, replaying the drama, you make it more real, more solid and increase the likelihood of it happening again. You are giving it power and actually recreating it in the present.

If you try and interfere with a scene that someone is acting out (replaying), you run various risks. One is that you validate their case, thus giving it your power. Another is that you may become part of the drama, cast in a role that you do not want. A third possibility is that you may invalidate the person who is in the replay because he or she knows that this behavior is not quite right, not quite coming from the true self. Counselors and therapists often try to get their clients to "talk this out." This is not only inadvisable but it serves to further activate the incident, driving the person further into it. The Dynamism clearing practitioner in a clearing session uses a very different technique that allows the [3]viewer to do knowingly what he is currently doing unknowingly, thus bringing the old incident into a new perspective and bringing it under the viewer's control.

The true self, the being, is senior to his case. This is why clearing can work at all. The practitioner and the viewer work together to clear the case, they form a team. In the early stages of clearing the practitioner can often see the spiritual being better than the individual himself, but as time goes on the person's spiritual strength improves. He becomes more certain of who he is and he can more easily see when he is being irrational, having inappropriate degrees of emotion or being self-righteous about some piece of case that he has figured out is right, noble, or in some way important to hang onto. We use

---

[2] Psychic Recording: Not a mental phenomenon, it is recorded in the Dynamis of the being.

[3] Viewer: A term used for a person having a clearing or coaching session.

our intellects to give us reasons why our idiosyncrasies are justifiable, why we are right to be jealous, mean or dislike some harmless soul on sight. We use this reasoning ability to strengthen our cases, which we believe will protect us from all evils. Nothing could be further from the truth. Some people have developed a talent for rationalizing away the most flagrantly unethical behavior, using up TONS of their reasoning capacity that could surely be used for some more profitable purpose.

All the evil we have experienced, perpetrated or witnessed is recorded in our cases. All the good is within our being. If you're unhappy, angry or have some other unwanted emotions, it is part of your case. Blame, regret, self-depreciation, self invalidation, all these are case manifestations resulting from some unrelieved, unresolved thought imprinted within your case and held there because you believe that in some way it is survival to do so.

[4]The being truly does not exist in the world of motion; therefore all case is a collection of lies and partial truths, altered truth and misunderstandings. This is why correcting false data is so effective. Every piece of case that is resolved removes some lies from the being that frees up his perceptions and abilities.

When events occur we record them in the form of psychic impressions and mental images. When later we think of these we re-create the image and impressions automatically. These impressions and superimpose themselves upon the physical universe and our bodies without our conscious awareness registering that they have done so.

Bringing a person to knowingly revisit these images and impressions desensitizes them for they are no longer hidden or partly hidden. For example: you know an event occurred but the details are hazy, this event is partially concealed from you. Because one tends to shy away from painful memories they are unlikely to be re-inspected unless your attention is specifically directed to the event or episode. This is where the Dynamis Clearing Practitioner comes in useful. He guides the being to actually contact and view the memories.

When one is reminded knowingly or subconsciously of the event, the energies stored within the memory may become activated and can then affect one's perception of the current events causing a cognitive dissonance between then and now. Unwanted sensations and emotions that are inappropriate to the current events turn on. Your first clue that this is happening is when you find yourself reacting with more emotion than the event really calls for, or see another "over-reacting." One is not really over-reacting; one is *reacting* to an earlier event that had some similarity to the present situation. This is why it is often so distressing to be told one is overreacting. It is not quite true; the truth is that you have your emotion *now* plus your emotion from *then*. This adds up to more than the situation at present warrants and blows it all out of proportion that can wreck relationships, businesses and marriages. This can really make a mess of one's entire life.

---

[4] For a more thorough explanation of the metaphysical concept behind this statement read my book "The Healing Spirit".

If a person can be brought to revisit and re-examine such an event, the forgotten information becomes available again. The emotion and energy, locked within it is able to flow again and eventually dissipates and becomes harmless.

Psychic Impression Clearing

There are two main types of psychic impression: **traumatic events** and **reminders of traumatic events**. One psychic impression can have literally thousands of reminders. A reminder serves to open a gateway to the old trauma allowing its energy to come into the present and affect the individual again. One can view the psychic impression and it becomes less devastating in its impact. One can view the reminders of the old impression and their energy dissipates so that the psychic impression drops out of sight allowing one to operate for a while without its influence. It is not gone but it is rendered temporarily impotent and it will never again have quite so much force. It can be reactivated again by the idea or perception that there is a similar danger in the environment. This type of clearing is called *deactivation*.

One can recreate the psychic impression fully; reliving it, which requires one to recreate knowingly that which one has been creating unknowingly and automatically. Since Dynamis is energy and has some existence within the physical realm, it falls under that law of physics that states that two objects cannot occupy the same space and time. When it is recreated it violates this condition and disappears as an energy construct becoming a memory like any other memory. This type of clearing is called *deletion or erasure*.

There are certain subjects that lock on to literally thousands of psychic impressions. One such subject is education; another is communication. One can work on these subjects directly, deleting thousands of these reminders as a byproduct. This causes many psychic impressions to become inert and the individual to become sharper, more alert, and generally feel better. Mis-defined words, for example, can produce tremendous relief once clarified, way beyond the amount of relief one would expect from simply defining a word correctly. This is because the mis-defined word was a keyword that prevented any flow in the area being addressed. The person would have said, "I can't think in this area." before the words were redefined. Addressing these subjects and clearing them up separates the individual from large numbers of psychic impressions and gives him the ability to learn in the area being addressed. This is called *subject clearing*.

There are certain psychic impressions and wounds that have inscribed themselves so deeply on the person's consciousness that they have gateways permanently open, causing the psychic impression to be in a state of almost continual activation.

The individual is usually unaware that this is happening but periodically flies into a storm of emotion that distresses him and those around him. Sometimes he may become aware of it afterwards. In some severe cases there is no recall of the storm except for a lingering sense of unreality or discomfort.

The psychic impression or wound in such a case superimposes itself on the current surroundings affecting the person's judgment and perceptions. It can seem to the individual to be more real than the actual reality. The mechanism that causes this is that in the present someone or something is close enough to the original event that the reminders are everywhere. They are keeping the impression alive and activating it continuously and repetitively.

If, for example, the original event or episode contained a violent explosion of wrath in which a woman was brutalized and physically hurt by a drunken man, any man who is not smiling, any person who is angry, shouting or intoxicated, a violent movie, loud voices, any or all of these could serve to reactivate the impression.

These impressions are tricky to access because the person is so accustomed to their presence that he thinks this is normal. He is used to feeling anxious inside and trying to conceal it. If he thinks about it at all he assumes everyone feels that way or that he is just that way and it cannot be changed. The impression surrounds him, superimposing itself on the environment and he sees life through it. When the circumstances approximate the original event too closely the person at once goes into high danger mode and starts reacting as though the original event is happening NOW. If the being is a high-powered being, the impression may catch those around him in his thrall and they will actually begin to act it out. This serves to convince the individual that the conclusions he drew in the original event are true. In examples given, the person decided: "Men are dangerous", and "Tempers are unpredictable." This reinforced the impression and gave it more and more power. The more frequently this happens, the more powerful it gets. The person does not see that his or her influence is actually creating events.

The Dynamis of the person contains the impression of the wound. As the Dynamis flows out from him it catches up those around him with its emotion and pattern. They react to this and begin to resonate according to the note it strikes. For example: He perceives them as potentially hostile and is ready to jump the least sign that there is hostility present. Sensing this, they in turn begin to feel hostile. They begin to act like the people in the original episode, making it seem as if these things *always* happen to him. He feels persecuted. He is sure HE did nothing to cause this. This new episode strengthens his belief that people are unpredictably hostile to him for no reason that he can see. He is unaware that he is causing a large part of it. He has become his own victim, the effect of his own causation.

Once an impression like this is found and cleared, the person's perception of the present becomes *much* clearer. The old repetitive pattern of events that he had been unknowingly creating ceases, and he is far more capable and able to create those things he really wants to create.

While we generally think of clearing away the old baggage from past wounds as intended for spiritual gain, it is also true that frees up the attention so that the person has more of its available when he wishes to concentrate on his business affairs. He has more horsepower. When he wants to create a friendly impression, he can do it. His ability to manifest what he wants becomes stronger. His thinking is clearer so he makes fewer mistakes. His attention is in the here and now, not locked up in the there and then.

Specific clearing can be used in business areas as well for reversals in business. Losses or errors one has made can result in the individual becoming overly cautious and otherwise impair his judgment in various ways. A person who has a psychic wound (a wound that damaged his trust and confidence, one which hit him squarely in one of his core beliefs or closely held principles) in the area of business or success will tend to form a pattern that is the opposite of the pattern on which he had been operating. So if he has been operating in a very confident manner he may decide that in the future he had better be more cautious and watchful. If, on the other hand, he has always been on the cautious side he will probably now become more reckless or he might decide to go towards being even more cautious and careful. In either case he changes rather drastically. He thinks his old operating basis has failed him, but instead of just adjusting it he makes a very sweeping change. His emotional state demands that.

Individuals know *intellectually* that they wish to change their attitudes. They also know the ideas and patterns they want to have, but *emotionally* deep down they believe they cannot. Even when a person affirms and asserts their optimistic beliefs over and over, the pattern formed at the time of the wound still comes into play when the person is under pressure. Clearing relieves this. All the affirmations in the world will not remove the earlier belief. It has been there so long it has grown roots.

Each individual has his own specific life energy that we call Dynamis. When a person has a psychic wound the anguish and emotion in that wound bleed out into the universe in his Dynamis, where eventually it is mirrored back at him causing him much distress. The person does not usually realize what he is emanating, for it is not what he is consciously intending. He thinks he is emanating friendliness and an encouraging attitude, and he is. The problem is that subliminally (under the surface) he is also emanating suspicion and caution. The emanations reflect back at him giving him mixed messages. People don't seem as trustworthy or nice. He doesn't realize that he is perceiving his own emotion reflecting back to him. Naturally, those with whom he is involved sense his distrust. In turn they distrust him, they like him less than they ordinarily would have, they feel rather cynical towards him. He is at a loss to explain this reaction.

When a person has experienced betrayal and loss, he tends to pick himself up and trudge forward; locking the feelings and pain away in some dark recess where he hopes they will not constantly bother him.

However, he *does* remember the conclusions he formed and his reasons behind them. It is the painful emotion and energy that he wishes to forget. Unfortunately these same emotions and energies are imprinted deeply and when even slightly similar circumstances occur, a gateway can open to them and that emotion and energy gush into the present, and he (or others) may think he is overreacting to the present circumstances. Actually he is reacting to the similarity to the old wound. Since these old wounds tend to fix emotional responses in set patterns they make the individual incapable of responding in the present with the appropriate degree of action and communication.

A psychic wound cuts very deeply. It actually can change the course of a person's very existence. Often a person swings wildly from one mindset to its opposite. This is called the pendulum effect. He was an atheist and he now becomes devout, or vice versa. What once seemed right now seems utterly wrong. Life is never as innocent and some of the magic is gone. Clearing the wound out of his Dynamis restores the magic without destroying the experience he gained. It removes the energy and emotion and allows the person to think more clearly in the area that has been cleared.

Naturally the most fertile ground for finding psychic wounds is in the area of personal relationships, but we tend to forget that business relationships can be just as painful, if not more so, because often losses in business effect our personal relationships and our family lives. Also success and prosperity are not really *just* physical universe manifestations.

There is prosperity and success of the spirit.

There is prosperity and success of the intellect and there is emotional prosperity and success.

Some people who are very successful in the material universe are extremely insecure emotionally or are unsatisfied intellectually.

Ideally one has a harmony of spiritual, emotional and physical prosperity and success. This is what Dynamis clearing can help you achieve. It is not an easy path, requiring courage and tenacity as well as the will to be the best you can possibly be. It takes courage for the individual to revisit and re-examine their worst nightmares and most painful memories, but only by doing so can one free up one's pent-up life force and restore a natural state of grace.

There are no shortcuts or magic pills that will transform a person to his full potential overnight. It takes hard work and diligent application. The goal of Dynamism Clearing is to reach personal sovereignty. It is illogical to expect to be transformed by some external factor. The practitioner is simply a guide helping you transform yourself. Personal sovereignty is found within your self. Clearing is a way to bring out the diamond within.

The search for the golden nuggets may seem material in nature, but really it is a spiritual quest. It leads to spiritual prosperity, and *that* leads to finding the truth within you. Knowing yourself is the essential ingredient to knowing what your golden nuggets are. Without it you cannot hope to find your true goals or be able to look at how these goals have mutated into your current existence. I am sure we've all seen the person whose true purpose is to help others having a very difficult time staying in the box of secretary or factory worker. They are often dragging home stray cats, dogs, people, or helping someone in need when they are already overloaded with work and responsibilities of their own. This person has failed to knowledge what he or she really wants to do, which results in being always torn between following his real purpose and doing what he has agreed to do or is being paid to do.

Once you know who you really are your true goals, your golden nuggets, become far easier to identify and acknowledge. The universe will mirror your soul. Increased prosperity, health and happiness follow.

As I said before, clearing is not the easiest of paths. The beast within yourself can be very challenging to look at, but it is an extremely rewarding path, filled with golden nuggets and paved with the golden sunshine that is your soul.

It may well be the only true path among the labyrinth of false solutions, the one that leads to personal sovereignty and a very fulfilling life.

Exercises for Chapter Twenty

1. What to do when someone is in the grips of a drama:

   _____
   _____
   _____
   _____
   _____
   _____
   _____
   _____
   _____

2. What to do if you sense you are acting out an old drama:

   _____
   _____
   _____
   _____
   _____
   _____
   _____
   _____
   _____
   _____

3. Give some examples of psychic wounds creating patterns that repeat over and over:

   _____
   _____
   _____
   _____
   _____
   _____
   _____
   _____
   _____
   _____

4. Give some examples of the pendulum effect:

   _____
   _____
   _____
   _____
   _____

Enid Vien

_____
_____
_____
_____
_____
_____
_____
_____
_____
_____
_____
_____
_____

Chapter Twenty-one
SUMMATION

I hope you have found some value in this book. It is based on principles of living spiritually in a materialistic world. I believe one can have one's cake and eat it too, for there is much beauty and grace in the world and prosperity allows one the time and resources to enjoy them.

Essentially I have written of the creative nature of humanity. Paradoxically this is our biggest asset and our biggest liability. We are always creating; we can do nothing else. We create marvelous symphonies, and atomic bombs. Sometimes our creations seem diabolical and sometimes sublime.

When our creations seem to take on a life of their own it can be exciting or terrifying. Often we identify ourselves with our creations or feel we have revealed our souls in a painting or poem. If we create something we consider bad or harmful all too often we refuse to create at all, we introvert and withdraw. We fail to notice that introversion and withdrawal is still a creation. We are always creating *something* even if it is just our own thoughts. Life itself seems to be a creative process. Some of us hold our creations too tightly and do not share them. I think this is an error. Fear of ridicule or criticism holds us back far too often.

I have written in the hopes of inspiring at least some of you to polish up your dreams and resurrect your talents. We are creative forces and our Golden Nuggets can help transform our lives and those of others.

You are your own pot of gold under your personal rainbow.

Enid Vien
La Mesa, Ca.
Oct 2000

Glossary

Accountability can be defined as those things for which one can be required to account.

Blame can be defined as the process of assigning fault

Core Belief: a belief that is central to the individual's thinking.

Duty can be defined as those things that are expected of one.

Dynamis Clearing: clearing out the tainted life energy so that the pure life force can flow freely.

Dynamism Clearing Practitioner: a person trained to guide you in clearing out your old decayed Dynamis.

Dynamism Coaching: learning to use your life energy to accomplish your goals more smoothly under the direction of a coach.

Dynamis: the life energy emanated by all living beings.

Dynamism: the study of life energy.

Givens: ideas that are so deeply accepted they elude inspection.

Golden Nuggets: You, your true goals, your own awareness. Those things that inspire you.

Off Purpose: following a goal that is not his own true purpose.

Pendulum effect: often after a psychic wound a person swings wildly from one mindset to its opposite.

Responsibility can be defined as the ability to control.

Righteous Computations: fixed ideas resulting from moments of chaos. These ideas fix us into patterns of behavior that seem helpful but actually trap us.

Self-fulfilling Prophecies: ideas that change the future, usually in the unwanted manner.

Viewer: the person viewing his own fixed patterns, psychic impressions or wounds in a Dynamis clearing session.

Other Books by Enid Vien:

The Healing Spirit

Scars on the Soul

Mood-Swings

Soul Mates: How To Find Them And Keep Them

For more information on Dynamism or to obtain books please write to:

Dynamism Publications
PO Box 242
La Mesa, CA. 91944-0242

Or visit our web site at:

www.dynamism.org